Music in Central Java

Music in Central Java

∞

EXPERIENCING MUSIC, EXPRESSING CULTURE

∞

BENJAMIN BRINNER

New York   Oxford
OXFORD UNIVERSITY PRESS
2008

Oxford University Press, Inc., publishes works that further Oxford University's
objective of excellence in research, scholarship, and education.

Oxford   New York
Auckland   Cape Town   Dar es Salaam   Hong Kong   Karachi
Kuala Lumpur   Madrid   Melbourne   Mexico City   Nairobi
New Delhi   Shanghai   Taipei   Toronto

With offices in
Argentina   Austria   Brazil   Chile   Czech Republic   France   Greece
Guatemala   Hungary   Italy   Japan   Poland   Portugal   Singapore
South Korea   Switzerland   Thailand   Turkey   Ukraine   Vietnam

Published by Oxford University Press, Inc.
198 Madison Avenue, New York, New York 10016
http://www.oup.com

Library of Congress Cataloging-in-Publication Data
Brinner, Benjamin Elon.
  Music in central Java : experiencing music, expressing culture / Benjamin
Brinner.
    p. cm. — (Global music series)
    Includes bibliographical references and index.
    ISBN 978-0-19-514736-0 (cloth : alk. paper) — ISBN 978-0-19-514737-7 (pbk. : alk.
paper)
    1. Music—Indonesia—Java—History and criticism. 2. Music—Social aspects—
Indonesia--Java. 3. Gamelan—Indonesia—Java. I. Title. II. Series.

ML345.I5B75 2007
780.9598'26—dc22   2006050652

Printing number: 9 8 7 6 5 4 3 2 1

Printed in the United States of America
on acid-free paper

GLOBAL MUSIC SERIES

General Editors: Bonnie C. Wade and Patricia Shehan Campbell

For my family near and far, Lisa, Maya, Omri, and Devon

Contents

Foreword

∞

In the past three decades interest in music around the world has surged, as evidenced in the proliferation of courses at the college level, the burgeoning "world music" market in the recording business, and the extent to which musical performance is evoked as a lure in the international tourist industry. This heightened interest has encouraged an explosion in ethnomusicological research and publication, including production of reference works and textbooks. The original model for the "world music" course—if this is Tuesday, this must be Japan—has grown old, as has the format of textbooks for it, either a series of articles in single multiauthored volumes that subscribe to the idea of "a survey" and have created a canon of cultures for study, or single-authored studies purporting to cover world musics or ethnomusicology. The time has come for a change.

This Global Music Series offers a new paradigm. Instructors can now design their own courses; choosing from a set of case study volumes, they can decide which and how much music they will teach. The series also does something else; rather than uniformly taking a large region and giving superficial examples from several different countries within it, case studies offer two formats—some focused on a specific culture, some on a discrete geographical area. In either case, each volume offers greater depth than the usual survey. Themes significant in each instance guide the choice of music that is discussed. The contemporary musical situation is the point of departure in all the volumes, with historical information and traditions covered as they elucidate the present. In addition, a set of unifying topics such as gender, globalization, and authenticity occur throughout the series. These are addressed in the framing volume, *Thinking Musically* (Wade), which sets the stage for the case studies by introducing those topics and other ways to think about how people make music meaningful and useful in their lives. *Thinking Musically* also presents the basic elements of music as they are practiced in musical systems around the world so that authors of each case study do not have to spend time explaining them and can delve immediately into the particular music. A second framing volume, *Teaching Music*

Globally (Campbell), guides teachers in the use of *Thinking Musically* and the case studies.

The series subtitle, "Experiencing Music, Expressing Culture," also puts in the forefront the people who make music or in some other way experience it and also through it express shared culture. This resonance with global studies in such disciplines as history and anthropology, with their focus on processes and themes that permit cross-study, occasions the title of this Global Music Series.

Bonnie C. Wade
Patricia Shehan Campbell
General Editors

Preface

EXPERIENCING MUSIC AND EXPRESSING CULTURE IN CENTRAL JAVA

In the middle of the archipelago of the Republic of Indonesia lies the island of Java. The central portion of the island, consisting of the province of Central Java and the special administrative district of Yogyakarta, is home to about a third of the densely populated island's 100 million residents. Here Javanese language is spoken and cultural practices understood to be ethnically Javanese are widespread. Although some fundamental concepts and practices of music, dance, and theater are shared the full length of the island, many are specific to the central area.

In this book I hope to communicate aspects of musical experience and cultural expression that have been widely shared in Central Java in recent decades. Many date back to the more distant past. The experience of music has many facets—some intensely personal, others shared among members of groups both small and large. Performers and listeners, for instance, tend to experience music differently. Sociocultural distinctions such as age, gender, economic standing, class, and ethnicity often foster different musical experiences. Conveying experience across such boundaries inevitably involves challenges of translation, challenges I encountered as I studied Javanese music and the musicians who make it.

Javanese gamelan music is often cited as an expression of the essence of Javanese culture, indeed of Javaneseness itself, not just as an identity but as a way of being. Much of this music is thought, for instance, to be effective in calming the mind and focusing the thoughts, highly valued goals around which various schools of Javanese spiritual practice have arisen. Performance of gamelan music has also been promoted as a way of learning quintessential aspects of personal refinement and proper Javanese conduct in social interaction.

Like any attempt to define the essence of a culture, such formulations are both enticing and problematic. In recent years the concept of monoethnic, geographically defined cultures has been challenged as historically inaccurate, because few societies have lived in isolation from other groups. Java is a case in point: In recent centuries ethnic Chinese (who have resided in Central Java for over four centuries) have performed and patronized "Javanese" arts, interaction with European traders and colonizers has influenced local arts in many ways, and contacts with musical practices from other parts of Southeast Asia, India, and the Middle East have all had an impact. Older concepts of culture have also proven to be increasingly out of touch with the realities of the contemporary world, with its massive rapid flows of people, ideas, and consumer goods, including recordings of music (Wade 2004: xiv–xv). The notion (promoted by earlier generations of anthropologists) that all parts of a culture form a tightly integrated package has come under attack, not least because of the tendency to present a static image of a culture, unchanging in time. Contemporary scholars have also shown how cultural traditions have been invented or manipulated to serve the interests of particular elites or other social forces.

A danger inherent to a book such as this is the production of a normative account of cultural practices, a set of rules and a story of conformity. Though I focus on integrative aspects of Javanese culture, the numerous connections that bind a set of practices and ideas, I also note elements that do not fit neatly into a "Javanese culture" package and point to instances of political manipulation of cultural practices.

THREE THEMES

Among the numerous significant aspects of Javanese music, three struck me as particularly important keys to understanding. Sufficiently abstract for generalizations and comparisons yet easily linked to specific phenomena, they will recur throughout this book. In brief, they are flexibility, appropriateness, and interconnectedness. *Flexibility* is inherent to both the frameworks of musical performance and the processes played out in a dialectical relationship with those frameworks. Musicians and their audiences make aesthetic judgments concerning the *appropriateness* of performers' choices with reference to specific performance contexts. However distinctive these contexts may be, they are linked in many ways, creating *interconnectedness*. Because Javanese arts are so deeply integrated, the connections between them set conditions for appropriateness and make demands on performers' flexibility. Thus, these three themes intersect: *Flexible* musical frameworks allow musicians to adapt pieces and musical processes to specific situations; they do so by choosing *appropriate* musical sound and behavior from the many *interconnected* possibilities. In principle these three themes are not uniquely Javanese, but they are manifested in specific ways that define

Javanese musical practices and traditions, distinguishing them from other types of music and ways of making music.

TERMINOLOGY AND PRONUNCIATION

Javanese musical terminology is abundant and unavoidable, and many concepts have no direct parallel in English. I have kept the number of terms to a minimum. All Javanese terms are italicized except gamelan and gong, because their use in English is frequent. I recommend savoring the onomatopoetic aspects of instrument names such as *kempul* and *kenong* as you say each word aloud according to the following brief guide to pronunciation:

C equals *ch* in church.
J equals *j* in judge.
G equals *g* in golf.
K equals *k* in kite, but it is a glottal stop in cases where it follows a vowel (e.g., *ayak-ayakan* is pronounced aya'-aya'an).
NG is a single sound, pronounced as in sing or ring (but never as in anger).
TH and DH represent retroflex sounds, distinct from *t* and *d*, produced by placing the tip of the tongue farther back than English speakers do for *t* and *d*. Sometimes the Javanese represent these sounds with a dot beneath the *d* or *t*, but some writings do not distinguish between them at all. Note that *th* is never pronounced like the English *th* in with or the.
Final A equals *aw* in awful. If the preceding vowel is an open *a*, then it is also pronounced *aw* (e.g., *pendhapa* is pronounced pendhawpaw). Sometimes the letter *o* is used instead (Solo rather than Sala).
E has three variants: 1) short and unaccented, 2) é pronounced like *ai* in paint, and 3) è pronounced like *ea* in dead.
I equals p*i*n in a closed syllable and (ending in consonant) s*ee* in an open syllable (ending in vowel).
O equals b*o*re in a closed syllable and zer*o* in an open syllable.
U equals p*u*t in a closed syllable and sh*oe* in an open syllable.
Older spellings may still be seen in names and some publications. These are the most important equivalents: oe = u, tj = c, dj = j, j = y.

ACKNOWLEDGMENTS

I owe my knowledge (but not my misunderstandings) of Javanese music and related arts to my teachers (listed by the names and titles they had when I studied with them): K.R.T. Wasitodiningrat, R. Ng. Martopangrawit, I.M. Harjito, Djoko Sungkono, R. Ng. Mloyowidodo, Martati, Suranto Atmosaputro, Midiyanto, Wakidi Dwidjomartono, and Heri Purwanto. Though I never had the opportunity to study with Hardja Susilo or Sumarsam, I learned from them what I could when I could. I have learned from other Javanese performers too numerous to mention, but would like to remember two who were particularly sweet in personality and playing: Pak Bei Tarnopangrawit, who played at the radio station and both Solonese palaces, and Pak Sular of Eromoko.

For their candid, helpful comments on drafts of the book I thank Sumarsam, Bonnie Wade, and Christina Sunardi. I owe thanks to Bonnie, too, for the opportunity to write this book and her willingness to put up with repeated delays, and to the editorial staff at Oxford University Press for their help and patience. I'd also like to thank the reviewers of the manuscript: David Harnish, Bowling Green State University; Ellen Koskoff, Eastman School of Music; R. Anderson Sutton, University of Wisconsin—Madison; and Sarah Weiss, Yale University.

This book would not have reached the form it has today without the substantial contributions of two people: Lisa Gold, with whom I have shared a family, a home, and professional life for two decades, and our dear friend Midiyanto who has inspired us time and again with his artistry and his generosity. Midiyanto directed the ensembles that performed most of the examples for this book and answered numerous questions as I worked on this book. Lisa tried out parts of the book in several classes. I am grateful to her students and mine for their feedback. Beyond (and before) that, Lisa led the way by writing *Music in Bali*, one of the first books in this series, and supported me in many ways through the arduous process of finishing this book.

CD Track List

All selections were recorded by Ben Brinner unless otherwise indicated.

1. "Dangdut: Begadang II," 0:29. Performed by Rhoma Irama. Smithsonian Folkways.

2. "Ada-ada Budhalan Mataraman," 1:20. Sung by Ki Sutino Hardokocarito with Hardo Budoyo, directed by Midiyanto. From performance of "Brajadenta Balela," 1991.

3. *Campursari* (excerpt), 0:40. Recorded at Midiyanto's house, Eromoko, 2000.

4. "Ladrang Lipursari" (beginning and end), 2:41. Recorded at R. Ng. Martopangrawit's house, Solo, 1983.

5. "Ladrang Sri Katon" (end), 1:07. Kraton Surakarta, Columbia Records, 1930(?).

6. "Ladrang Kembang Lintang" (excerpt), 1:48. *Gamelan sekatèn*, played by R. Ng. Martopangrawit and students, 1983.

7. "Ladrang Asmaradana" (beginning), 0:58. *Siter* ensemble led by Paimin Padmomintargo, 1993.

8. Gong forging, 0:20. Gongsmiths at Tentrem Sarwanto's workshop, 1993.

9. "Ladrang Asmaradana" (beginning & end), 1:12. Hardo Budoyo, directed by Midiyanto, 2000.

10. "Ketawang Subakastawa," 3:01. Hardo Budoyo, directed by Midiyanto, 2000.

11. *Lancaran* colotomic pattern, 0:16. Ben Brinner & Lisa Gold, Berkeley, 2006.

12. Individual gongs, 0:22. Ben Brinner & Lisa Gold, Berkeley, 2006.

13. "Lancaran Singa Nebah Pélog," 0:28. Hardo Budoyo, directed by Midiyanto, 2000.

14. *Ladrang* colotomic pattern, 0:30. Ben Brinner & Lisa Gold, Berkeley, 2006.

15. *Ciblon* strokes, 0:20. Midiyanto, 2000.

16. *Ciblon* pattern 1, 0:32. Midiyanto, 2000.

17. *Ciblon* pattern 2, 0:34. Midiyanto, 2000.

18. *Lancaran* drum pattern with colotomic instruments, 1:30. Midiyanto, Lisa Gold, Ben Brinner, 2006.

19. "Lancaran Singa Nebah Pélog," 3:46. Hardo Budoyo, directed by Midiyanto, 2000.

20. "Lancaran Bèndrong" & "Gangsaran," 1:39. Gamelan Sari Raras, directed by Heri Purwanto and Ben Brinner, 2004.

21. "Talu," 8:54. Hardo Budoyo, directed by Midiyanto, 2000.

22. *Sléndro* & *pélog* scales, 0:46. Lisa Gold, Berkeley, 2006.

23. *Sléndro* & *pélog* compared 1, 0:17. Hardo Budoyo, directed by Midiyanto, 2000.

24. *Sléndro* & *pélog* compared 2, 0:23. Hardo Budoyo, directed by Midiyanto, 2000.

25. "Ladrang Asmaradana" featuring individual instruments, 3:38. Hardo Budoyo, directed by Midiyanto, 2000.

26. "Lancaran Singa Nebah Sléndro," 5:14. Hardo Budoyo, directed by Midiyanto, 2000.

27. "Ladrang Asmaradana" (excerpt), 6:07. Hardo Budoyo, directed by Midiyanto, 2000.

28. "Macapat Pucung," 0:38. Midiyanto, Berkeley, 2006.

29. "Ketawang Subakastawa Pélog Nem," 5:11. Hardo Budoyo, directed by Midiyanto, 2000.

30. *Gendèr* and *gambang* elaboration, 1:09. Heri Purwanto & Midiyanto, 2003.

31. Voices of *wayang kulit* characters: Arjuna, Cakil, Bima, Kresna, Semar, Banowati, Gathutkaca, Brajadenta, 1:13. Midiyanto, Berkeley, 2006.

32. "Gendhing Kabor," "Ayak-ayakan Nem," & "Pathetan Nem Wantah," 5:27. Ki Sutino Hardokocarito with Hardo Budoyo, directed by Midiyanto. From performance of "Brajadenta Balela," 1991.

33. "Srepeg Nem" & "Ada-ada Nem," 3:42. Ki Sutino Hardokocarito with Hardo Budoyo, directed by Midiyanto. From performance of "Brajadenta Balela," 1991.

Musicians who participated in the Hardo Budoyo performance of "Brajadenta Balela" in 1991: Sutino Hardokocarito (*dhalang*), Supini (*pesindhèn*), Wakidi Dwidjomartono (*kendhang*), Midiyanto (*rebab* and *demung*), Sularto (*gendèr*), Darso, Sugiyono, Tugiman, Sukarno, Kuswanto, Wakino, Sutini, Ben Brinner, Alex Dea, Lisa Gold, Kitsie Emerson, Richard Wallis.

Musicians who participated in the Hardo Budoyo recordings in 2000: Darsi and Sri Sularni (*pesindhèn*), Midiyanto, Giman, Hendro Supeno, Himawan, Midi Sumur, Paiman, Samijo, Saminu, Sitri Plecing, Sugiyono, Sularto, Sulastri, Suliyo, Sumarno, Suranto, Suratno.

CHAPTER 1

First Hearings

INTRODUCTION

Flying in to any of the airports in Central Java, one passes a string of majestic volcanic peaks. These form the backbone of the 1,100-mile-long island of Java. Even when the rest of the densely populated island is shrouded in clouds, the 9,000-foot peaks stand out in the sun. This aerial vantage point gives little sense of how life looks, feels, sounds, or smells on the ground, but it does reveal the overall structure of the island—the lay of the land that has shaped human history—and it highlights the volcanic sources from which both agricultural fertility and periodic destruction have flowed. As an introductory text for non-Javanese readers, this book must give you an aerial view of Javanese culture, a figurative "lay of the land," or you will not know which way is north (a Javanese figure of speech that indicates utter confusion). At the same time, this distanced view must be offset by "on-the-ground" descriptions of culture in performance in order to give a sense of how music and allied performing arts are experienced by Javanese performers and audiences.

Between two volcanoes in a broad, hot valley filled with rice fields, villages, and small towns lies Surakarta (see figure 1.1). This sprawling city of over half a million, situated on the Solo River, is commonly called Solo. A center of Central Javanese cultural life since the eighteenth century, it is the site of two rival royal palaces, one just south of the center of town, and the other a short distance to the northwest. The city also hosts a performing arts conservatory for high school students and one of the most important arts academies in Indonesia. These institutions draw musicians, dancers, and shadow play performers from surrounding areas and many other parts of Indonesia. In turn, the academy, conservatory, and government radio station supply music, theater, and dance to surrounding areas through live performances, broadcasts, and recordings.

Solo is widely regarded as the site of the most refined aspects of Javanese traditional culture, including language and the performing arts. It has not figured as prominently in national politics as the rival

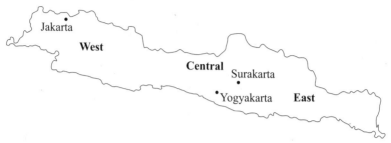

FIGURE 1.1 *Map of Java showing the two court cities of Central Java, Surakarta and Yogyakarta, and the capital of Indonesia, Jakarta.*

court city to the southwest, Yogyakarta (pronounced Jogjakarta and often abbreviated to Yogya or Jogja), nor is it a major hub of economic activity. Most foreigners visit Yogya, which has been developed as a major tourist destination. Those who do reach Solo have tended to come for lengthy stays in order to study Javanese performing arts or Javanese mysticism and meditation. Aside from some short periods of rioting and expressions of anti-American sentiment, Solo has been a relatively quiet city that shades off into a patchwork of suburbs and villages engulfed in urban sprawl. Shopping malls and a few multistory buildings have changed the profile of the city in the past twenty years, but open-air markets continue to be an important part of its fabric.

The streets, dry and dusty much of the year, are traversed by uniformed students from secular and Muslim schools, government clerks, villagers coming to sell produce, market vendors, and businesspeople. They are filled with far more motorcycles, small public transport vans, and pedicabs than private cars. Food vendors announce their presence with special sounds as they wheel or carry their wares through the streets: A high-pitched call announces a baked goods cart, a metal spoon banging a china bowl signals soup with fish balls, and a soft, low steam whistle lets people know that a delicious steamed sweet is coming their way. These sounds mix with Indonesian and Javanese music tapes blaring from houses and roadside cassette stalls. Occasionally an itinerant musician or two will add to the sonic soup, hoping to be paid a few cents to play a song or to be silent and move on.

Much of the music disseminated over the air and via cassettes and disks is Indonesian pop. Played mainly on instruments such as electric guitar, bass, and synthesizers, it is related to Indian and Western popular music practices in terms of its sounds, its song subjects and structures, and its commercial system, including star singers such as Rhoma Irama

(CD track 1). Song texts are usually in Indonesian rather than Javanese, and the songs are widespread throughout the country.

Gamelan music is also commonly audible on the airwaves and in the streets of Central Java, particularly at night when radios at all-night food stalls often are tuned to stations broadcasting performances of shadow plays in which gamelan music is a central component (CD track 2). Such plays are a vital component of major life cycle events and a common form of civic celebration. To some extent Indonesian pop and Javanese gamelan are two discrete sound worlds, with radically different aesthetics, meanings, and patterns of production and consumption. This book focuses on the long-standing gamelan tradition, which sometimes intersects with Indonesian popular music. The most recent of these intersections, *campursari*, mixes the instruments and musical practices of gamelan with those of Indonesian popular music (CD track 3).

> **ACTIVITY 1.1** *Write a brief essay comparing tracks 1, 2, and 3. Try to capture the differences in singing style and in the use of instruments to accompany the voice. You can continue the comparison by listening to several tracks on* Music of Indonesia, vol. 2 *(see Resources; brief excerpts are available at www.folkways. si.edu). Write a paragraph comparing the sound to other kinds of music that you know. How would you characterize the different sounds of* kroncong *and* dangdut?

WHAT IS A GAMELAN?

The word *gamelan* refers not to a particular instrument but to an ensemble, which may range from a handful of instruments to a very large set. Most of the instruments in a gamelan are idiophones with a metal sounding element, shaped as either round gongs or slab-like keys. The preferred metal is bronze, cast and forged by hand; brass and iron are cheaper but sonically inferior alternatives. Drums, bowed and plucked strings, a xylophone, and end-blown flutes round out the ensemble.

Some gamelan instruments are centuries old, prized heirlooms that are venerated as repositories of spiritual power and symbols of status and wealth. They may be given offerings of flowers and incense. Some are newer and larger, lacking special symbolic or spiritual significance, while others are downright plain and utilitarian. They are often created as a set under the guidance of one maker and owned as a set by an individual or institution. Unlike musicians in many other cultures, Javanese musicians often do not own instruments of their own but go to play on whichever gamelan set is being used for a particular performance.

GAMELAN PERFORMANCE CONTEXTS IN SOLO: LIFE CYCLES AND MUSICAL CYCLES

Gamelan music is played in a wide variety of settings for various purposes, including entertainment, ritual, education, meditation, or commemoration of special occasions. It is often performed as an integral part of shadow plays and other types of theater or as an accompaniment to dance. In this chapter you will get a sense of this variety through a brief tour of some of the places and contexts in which I have heard or performed gamelan. In subsequent chapters you will learn more about several of these contexts and come to appreciate how the music and its significance vary from one context to another.

A few months into my first stay in Java, my teacher, Radèn Ngabehi Martopangrawit (hereafter Pak Marto), invited me to a celebration of his daughter's birthday. This was a special birthday, marking the completion of her first eight years, one of the longest cycles in the calendrical complex so important to most Javanese. Pak Marto marked the occasion at his house with a *klenèngan*, a performance of gamelan music in its own right (i.e., not as part of a dance or theater performance). Food and drink were served to both guests and musicians throughout the evening.

The house was modest, located behind a low wall topped by an iron railing on a quiet street in one of the many neighborhoods of Solo. The single-story dwelling, with tile roof atop concrete walls, blended with its neighbors. As in most such houses, the front door opened into a small room lined with chairs for receiving guests. Passing through this, one reached the main room, devoid of chairs. Here were the few instruments that Pak Marto owned. Some were gifts from foreign students, others gifts from the government in recognition of his accomplishments as a musician and teacher. It was here that I had my lessons twice a week, seated cross-legged on a woven mat on the tile floor.

For the birthday *klenèngan*, the entire tile floor had been covered with mats and the instruments of a small gamelan filled about half the room. This was a "chamber" ensemble, a *gamelan gadhon*, which consists mainly of the quieter gamelan instruments on which the more elaborate parts are played. The evening was a real musical treat as the focus was on the refined elaborations of some fine musicians, Pak Marto's students and colleagues from the performing arts academy. The adult guests, roughly equal in number to the musicians, sat around the edges of the room, eating, chatting, and listening to the music while children played in an adjacent room. In the course of the evening, a number of long pieces were played singly or strung together in medleys. One of the medleys consisted of almost an hour and a half of uninterrupted music. It included numerous contrasts of tempo and texture, all performed with refined smoothness by the choice group of musicians. The sequence of pieces conformed to conventions of modal order and alternation between two different tunings, each played on a separate set of instruments. The only disruption to this expected order occurred when Pak Marto called his daughter into the room, made a brief speech, and then had the musicians play the short piece after which he had named her. This was Lipursari, meaning "essence of comfort," a fitting name for Pak Marto's youngest daughter, the child of his old age (CD track 4 consists of the beginning and end of this piece).

Through one of the guests at Pak Marto's celebration, I obtained an invitation to another celebration. Although this was also a life-cycle ritual, the contrast could hardly have been greater. Instead of an intimate musical gathering, I found an ostentatious display of wealth as the owners of one of the best-known fabric stores celebrated the circumcisions of their two sons with a *wayang kulit* (shadow play; hereafter abbreviated to *wayang*).

Drawn by the sound of gamelan and the amplified voice of the *dhalang* (puppet master), hundreds of people thronged the street outside the guarded gate to the courtyard of an opulent house. Some climbed the outer wall to watch the show. A printed invitation got me past the gate, though as one of the few foreigners in Solo, I probably would have been admitted in any case since the presence of foreign guests would elevate the status of the event and the hosts. The courtyard was filled with rows of chairs for hundreds of male guests. I was directed to the handful of male guests seated near the musicians on a raised platform in front of the house. Female guests were escorted into the house. The glass doors had been removed from the front room to make way for a large white cloth screen stretched on an ornately carved wooden frame. This effectively separated the men from the women, although its primary purpose was to serve as the "stage" on which puppets' shadows would be projected.

The *dhalang*, seated cross-legged facing the screen, was just beginning the performance as I arrived. In a sonorous voice he narrated the opening scene, using language that would become increasingly familiar as I attended more *wayang* performances. Though the details would change from one show to the next according to the dramatic needs of the specific story, the main themes of this narration, and indeed most of the specific phrases, would recur in other *dhalangs'* narrations. I would hear most of the same music, too, in other *wayang* performances, varying a bit with the story and the musicians' abilities.

As the evening wore on, guests who had attended more out of social obligation than out of a desire to watch *wayang* got up and left. The formality that had prevailed during the first scenes was relaxed both on screen and off as the facade of Muslim propriety faded: the gender segregation of the audience broke down and alcoholic drinks began to circulate. The action on the screen became livelier, with jokes from the *dhalang* answered by raucous laughter and occasional catcalls from the musicians and audience. The guests who left early missed the nuances and plot twists of the particular performance, but they probably did not need to stay to know how the story ended because it was an episode from the Mahabharata, an epic cycle originally brought from India. The Hindu gods and heroes who populate these stories are known to all, regardless of religious belief. Their presence at the celebration of a Muslim life-cycle event was not unusual at all.

From Hindu–Buddhist Java to the Advent of Islam. *This mix of Hindu and Muslim elements is but one of the many complexities of Javanese history. Massive stone structures dating back over a thousand years bear witness to the extensive import of Indian ideas over a period of several centuries that ended in the tenth century CE. Borobudur, near Yogyakarta, is a monument built around 800 CE that encases an entire hill in stone with sculpted panels that expound Buddhist teachings and worldview. Driving from Yogya to Solo, one passes the Prambanan, a large temple complex honoring the Hindu god Shiva that dates from the ninth and tenth centuries. Numerous smaller temples attest to the presence of a large, powerful Hindu-Buddhist kingdom in this area up to the tenth century. The nature of the connection to India is a subject of debate. There does not appear to have been any direct South Asian conquest or rule over Java, but the influence of Indian religion, language, writing, literature, law, art, dance, and architecture is undeniable. Sanskrit words constitute a significant portion of the Javanese literary vocabulary and personal names. Traditional Javanese script, now displaced by Roman letters, evolved from South Indian Pallava script. Javanese versions of the Indian Ramayana and Mahabharata epics persist to this day, in oral and written forms, as the main sources of theatrical plots. Song texts are still*

drawn from these sources. Certain dance postures show Indian influence, but musically there appear to be few (if any) Indian traces.

Evidence of the non-Indian aspects of Javanese life is more abundant in beliefs and practices than in concrete buildings. This includes beliefs both in local spirits to which offerings are made and in the concentration of spiritual energy in certain spots or beings from which power can be drawn. Like many other places in Southeast Asia, the opposition between mountain and sea is fundamental to traditional Javanese worldview. The animistic and Hindu aspects combine in exorcistic shadow plays that incorporate Hindu gods but propitiate local spirits in order to bring peace and prosperity to a community.

After the construction of Borobudur, Prambanan, and other religious monuments, political power shifted from Central to East Java. From the eleventh to the fifteenth century, the Majapahit Empire ruled over Java, Bali, and other parts of the archipelago that is now Indonesia. Its influence extended as far as mainland Southeast Asia. Majapahit retains a central place in the Javanese cultural imagination and hence in Javanese performing arts. While the Indian-derived Mahabharata and Ramayana of an earlier era predominate in theater and dance, the indigenous tales of Majapahit are also widely known and represented. In the nineteenth and twentieth centuries, both Dutch colonial scholars and Javanese aristocrats glorified Majapahit as the greatest flowering of Hindu-Javanese culture. A few particularly venerable musical instruments and daggers are said to be the product of Majapahit's smiths.

Majapahit was defeated around 1500 CE by the neighboring Muslim Javanese kingdom of Demak. It is important to note that Islam, like Hinduism and Buddhism, came to Java not by conquest from abroad but by gradual penetration through trade and other connections. It spread to include almost all the inhabitants of Java, at least nominally. Arabic words entered Javanese vocabulary and Islamic thought became influential. Although the call to prayer heard from mosques all over Java is Middle Eastern in melodic style, this style does not appear to have directly influenced gamelan music. Islam did not entirely displace Hinduism, Buddhism, and animism. While some Javanese became orthodox Muslims, others developed syncretic beliefs and practices. This was apparent (and still is) in both the villages and the courts. Origin myths point to both Hindu gods and Muslim saints as creators of gamelan instruments and music as well as wayang.

At the royal courts a gamelan is not just a set of instruments but an heirloom, a symbol of the court's might, and a repository of spiritual power. The major court in Solo, Kraton Surakarta, owns several centuries-old sets of instruments, each with its own name, history, and sound. The palace is closed off from the world behind high walls. Gaining access to performances there is not a simple matter, but if one knows the musicians, it is possible to attend rehearsals and broadcasts, which take place in several pavilions within this large palace complex.

One of my favorite places to hear gamelan is the other palace in Solo, the Istana Mangkunagaran. It has fewer sets of instruments but is more open to the public. At weekly rehearsals and monthly broadcasts, the beautiful instruments of an old gamelan dating back to the eighteenth century are played on the marble floor of an immense pavilion (*pendhapa*) so high that birds drift in and out, as you can hear in recordings made there ("Ketawang Puspawarna" track 8 on CD in Wade 2004). The gamelan consists of many gongs of various sizes, some hanging from ornately carved racks and others resting on ropes stretched over carved wooden boxes. Next to these is a long row of metallophones, each with seven bronze keys resting on carved wooden troughs and struck with hard wooden mallets. At one end are most of the softer instruments: a bowed lute, two sets of metallophones played with padded mallets, and a set of xylophones (one musician per set). A large zither and a flute are placed close by, and so are the male singers, in a semicircle in front of the drummer, who presides over the whole ensemble from a spot in the middle. The female singers kneel in a row at the very front. Some of them are trained as dancers, too. At least once a week, court dancers rehearse with gamelan accompaniment, their reflections gleaming on the Italian marble floor. The dancers often include older women who are passing their knowledge of the complex court dance repertoire on to young dancers, many from the performing arts academy.

Pendhapa structures are common at the entrance to the homes of nobility and in the royal palaces. In recent years they have been built at government and commercial sites as well. Attuned to the climate, they feature a smooth tile or concrete floor raised several feet above the ground. The structure generally has a wall only on one side, if at all. Square or rectangular, the *pendhapa* is covered by a high peaked roof supported on columns around the edge (see figure 1.2). A second set of columns closer to the center is also common, particularly for large pavilions. The Mangkunagaran *pendhapa* is so immense that it has an additional set of columns to support the roof and the central columns are unusually high. These structures stay cool in the daytime. The ceiling,

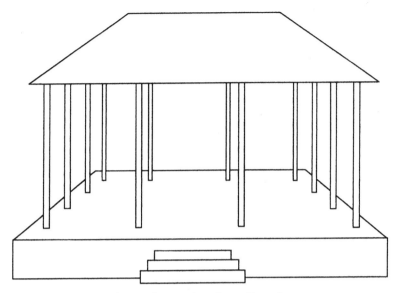

FIGURE 1.2A   *Pavilions: Schematic view of a small* pendhapa.

sloping down on all sides, collects and then diffuses the sound of the gamelan so that it can seem to float in the air, barely anchored to the actual instruments.

At both palaces gamelan performances are held whenever a royal occasion requires. The Mangkunagaran also presents commissioned performances for tour groups. While large royal events are no longer frequent, gamelan is still played every 35 days to mark the ruler's birth (whether he is present or not). All palace performances regularly begin with the signature piece of that particular court. "Ladrang Sri Katon" is played at the Kraton Surakarta (CD track 5 is the end of a recording from the early 1930s), while the Mangkunagaran musicians honor their prince with "Ketawang Puspawarna," written by one of his ancestors.

Colonial Rule.   *How is it that two courts exist within one city? This rivalry has had far-reaching effects on Javanese performing arts. It originated during the time of European imperialism. After the fall of the Majapahit Empire, a series of smaller kingdoms rose and fell as the center of Javanese power shifted back to Central Java. The last large Javanese empire, Mataram, arose around 1600 in the area where Yogyakarta now stands. It never equaled Majapahit*

FIGURE 1.2B *Pavilions in the palace of Yogyakarta with attendant in traditional court attire. (Photo by Ben Brinner.)*

in size and influence because of the arrival of European trade companies that saw the north coast of Java as a valuable foothold for protecting their trade routes to the Spice Islands east of Java. The Portuguese came first but were soon driven out by the Dutch. The main traces of Portuguese presence in the area are certain words and the musical genre kroncong, *which is thought to be a local adaptation of elements of Portuguese music.*

Dutch military and political influence grew throughout the eighteenth century, ending autonomous Javanese rule by the end of that century. Intervening in a conflict between contenders for the Javanese throne, the Dutch helped the uncle of the king in Surakarta to establish Yogyakarta as a rival court. As part of the 1755 treaty establishing this arrangement and putting an end to civil war, royal heirlooms, including gamelans, were divided between the two courts. Another rebellious branch of the royal family was pacified a few years later by the establishment of the Mangkunagaran palace in Surakarta, named after its prince, Mangkunagara. When the English ruled Java briefly during the Napoleonic wars, (1811–1816) they installed a fourth offshoot of the royal family in a rival court (the Pakualaman) in Yogykarta. Thus four royal courts, two headed by kings and two by princes, vied with one another.

The Dutch government asserted full colonial rule over Java after the English left. They sought to control the populace and extract as much profit as possible, particularly from the plantations they established. They supported Javanese courts as centers of feudal pomp and royal display without real political power.

Among the heirlooms divided between the first two rival courts (the Kratons in Surakarta and Yogyakorta) were the massive instruments of the *gamelan sekatèn*. Played every year for the celebration of the prophet Muhammad's birth (*Mulud*), this special type of gamelan consists of two halves. Each court obtained half of the original ensemble and had a second matching half made. The two halves are placed in pavilions on either side of the courtyard of the great mosque outside the palace and played in alternation throughout the day for two weeks, pausing only for the daily prayers, which are announced from the mosque.

Unlike most Javanese ensembles, the *gamelan sekatèn* includes neither singers nor the softer instruments featured in most other types of gamelan. These are the largest Javanese instruments, loudest and lowest in pitch (CD track 6). Yet nowadays you might not hear them until you were very close because during the holiday the area outside the mosque is an open-air market filled with the cacophonous play of various popular musics over distorted sound systems.

These spiritually charged heirlooms are brought to the mosque's courtyard in a special procession at the beginning of the holiday and returned at its end. This serves as a public display of emblems of the power of the royal court. Giant mountains of rice decorated with other foods are the centerpieces of these processions marking one of the most important Muslim holy days. These are not Muslim symbols but part of the common ritual language of Southeast Asia and evidence of animist beliefs. Both the instruments and the music played on them are potent signifiers. Despite the ongoing prestige of this music, there are no longer enough court musicians to play both sets, so students from the performing arts academy have been called in over the past few decades to supplement them.

CYCLICITY AND COINCIDENCE

While performances of the *gamelan sekatèn* are tied to the Muslim calendar, many other ritual celebrations involving music are linked to other calendrical cycles. I noted above that each royal court marks the reigning prince's birth once every 35 days with a gamelan concert. Less exalted individuals may also choose to mark their birthday with a performance. At its simplest, this could be a gathering in a private home with gamelan playing and friends seated on mats on the floor like Pak Marto's *klenèngan* described above. A few can afford to put on a substantial display. When I lived in Solo, one of the most famous shadow puppet masters in Java, Anom Soeroto, hosted shadow plays by other performers at his house in Solo, providing not only entertainment but dinner and other refreshments to the hundreds who showed up to this open event, which recurred every 35 days.

Why 35 days? This marks the coincidence of 5- and 7-day weeks, two of the many calendrical cycles that play important roles in Javanese lives (recall the eight-year cycle Pak Marto marked for his daughter). When a child is born, parents take as careful note of the particular intersection of the 5- and 7-day weeks as of the year. This intersection will recur every 35 days (after five 7-day weeks or seven 5-day weeks). For astrological calculations this intersection is of paramount importance, influencing decisions such as when a person moves or marries (and even the choice of an appropriate mate). Several other overlapping calendrical cycles may be taken into account as well (see Becker and Becker 1981: 209).

It is this attention to cyclicity and to the coincidence of different cycles that led Judith Becker to propose a homology between Javanese calendrical systems and gamelan music, where the coincidence of cycles is also tremendously important (1979; also presented in Becker and Becker 1981). Within these musical cycles there are also points of melodic convergence.

ACTIVITY 1.2   *Try to follow some of the individual strands in the rich musical texture of CD track 4. After the solo introduction you will hear one full cycle, lasting from the gong stroke at 0:13 to the next gong stroke at 1:34. Do you hear moments of coincidence when several melodies converge on the same pitch? When "Ladrang Lipursari" ends at 1:57—about twelve minutes of music were deleted from the middle of the recording due to lack of space—four of the musicians play another kind of piece, a* pathetan, *that is not cyclical. Do you hear melodic coincidence? Do the instrumental parts sound as tightly coordinated as in* "Ladrang Lipursari"?

The calendrical homology is not complete because Javanese musical cycles are exclusively measured in powers of 2, which leads to frequent coincidences and reinforcements of cycles rather than the singular coincidence of the 5- and 7-day cycles, which have no common denominator (see figure 1.3). The 8-year *windhu* that Pak Marto celebrated for his daughter is a relatively unusual unit of time, whereas cycles of five and seven are constantly in use. The idea of coincidence that Becker identifies, however, is a powerful organizing principle in Javanese music, and the desire to find meaningful patterns and numerical correspondences between different aspects of life is widespread in Javanese culture.

Other types of occasions may also be marked by performances. Weddings often feature dancers, accompanied by live gamelan or a recording. Often the dance will be a love duet, either choreographed as an independent dance or taken as an excerpt from one of the many dance dramas current in the Javanese theater. Other life-cycle rituals that may involve gamelan performance include a ceremony marking the seventh month of pregnancy, circumcision (for Muslim boys), and birthdays. Banks and other large businesses may sponsor a performance to mark the opening of a new branch. Municipalities and neighborhood associations sometimes sponsor gamelan, with or without shadow play, for Indonesian Independence Day (August 17).

Some rituals of a more religious or spiritual nature may also involve gamelan. The first day of the Javanese year is such an occasion. The courts mark it by perambulations of sacred heirlooms rather than with music, but elsewhere it may be celebrated with a *wayang* (see chapter 6). Another particularly important type of ritual performance is the relatively short *wayang* performed to exorcize, to safeguard from evil, or to ritually cleanse a person, group, or village.

MUSIC IN THE EVERYDAY

Music may also serve far more prosaic purposes. Children learn to play simple gamelan pieces in schools. Some continue to play when they grow up. Numerous amateur gamelan groups provide a regular social occasion for people to gather and chat, improving their playing skills a little and perhaps performing once in a while for small functions or competing in gamelan competitions. Such groups tend to be gender-segregated. They are often sponsored by a large government office or business for its employees and directed by a professional musician. In such groups, faithful rendition of the model presented by the teacher is expected rather than the spontaneity and limited individual freedom more typical of

1 2 3 4 5 **1** 2 3 4 5 **1** 2 3 4 5 **1** 2 3 4 5 **1** 2 3 4 5 **1** 2 3 4 5 **1** 2 3 4 5 **1**
1 2 3 4 5 6 7 **1** 2 3 4 5 6 7 **1** 2 3 4 5 6 7 **1** 2 3 4 5 6 7 **1** 2 3 4 5 6 7 **1**

A. Cycles of 5 and 7 coincide once every 35 units (5 x 7 or 7 x 5).

1 2 **1** 2 **1** 2 **1** 2 **1** 2 **1** 2 **1** 2 **1** 2 **1** 2 **1** 2 **1** 2 **1** 2 **1** 2 **1** 2 **1** 2 **1** 2 **1**
1 2 3 4 **1** 2 3 4 **1** 2 3 4 **1** 2 3 4 **1** 2 3 4 **1** 2 3 4 **1** 2 3 4 **1** 2 3 4 **1**
1 2 3 4 5 6 7 8 **1** 2 3 4 5 6 7 8 **1** 2 3 4 5 6 7 8 **1** 2 3 4 5 6 7 8 **1**
B. Cycles of 2 and 4 coincide every 4 units, cycles of 4 and 8 coincide every 8, etc.

FIGURE 1.3 *Coincidences between cycles of differing lengths.*

other performance contexts. The female groups almost invariably have a male teacher who may call in male musicians to fill in the lead parts for performances because relatively few women play these instruments.

Street musicians circulate in some areas, playing and singing at food stalls and entrances to buildings. Some play tambourine or guitar, but others play a *siter*, a small box zither, on which they pluck out two or three strands of the much more complex musical texture that would be played on a full gamelan. The *siter* player either sings while playing or performs with a singer. Some of them only seem to be interested in making enough noise to get somebody to give them a little money. But others, such as those heard on CD track 7, are competent musicians. When I recorded these brothers, they had become prominent musicians, playing at the radio station and in the courts, but they had started out as itinerant *siter* players, a social position little better than that of beggar. A few generations ago this was a more common—and perhaps less lowly—profession. Small ensembles including several other instruments besides a *siter* would perform in the street or courtyards of houses, often accompanying a female dancer.

PATRONAGE AND SOCIOPOLITICAL CHANGE

The period stretching from the late nineteenth century to the eve of World War II is widely viewed as a golden age of Javanese arts due to the amount of resources and attention lavished on theater, dance, and gamelan by the rulers in all four courts as they sought to outdo one another and to create individual styles that would mark each court's identity in the arts. The palaces supported hundreds of musicians and dancers, with an array of shadow masters also at their command. Elaborate displays of theater, dance, and music were presented on numerous occasions. The Javanese nobility also cultivated music and dance as essential to the education of the proper aristocrat. At this time, too, entrepreneurs of Chinese descent formed theater troupes and started commercial performances for the masses.

One of the more remarkable aspects of this period was the close interaction between Javanese and Europeans at the courts. Celebrations that involved Dutch colonial administrators often included both European and Javanese music and dance, with certain court musicians specializing in European instruments and music. Dutch scholars took a deep interest in the arts and found certain Javanese aristocrats to be willing partners in their investigations. Both Javanese and Europeans contributed articles to periodicals devoted to Javanese culture, often emphasizing ancient connections to India. One result of these interactions was a shift in the sorts of stories represented in the *wayang*, a rediscovery of Indian roots, as historian Laurie Sears has shown (1996). Another very different result was the development of several systems of musical notation as European concern over cultural change gave rise to fear that compositions might be lost due to the vagaries of oral transmission.

Social Status, Language, and Interaction.   As a feudal society, the Javanese developed a deep sense of hierarchy. The nobility held itself distinct from the common folk and paid extensive attention to distinctions of rank, elaborating these distinctions through dress, titles, perquisites, and language. Knowledge of gamelan was considered an important part of a noble's education, but public performance in a gamelan group was not. It was more acceptable for nobles to perform as dancers. Gamelan musicians were drawn from hereditary families of court musicians and from people outside the courts, in the cities and villages. A few musicians rose to ranks of nobility due to their achievements. Ranks, titles, and other trappings of aristocratic hierarchy are greatly attenuated today but are still evident in various ways, not least in theater.

The elaboration of status distinctions went hand in hand with linguistic developments. Over the course of several centuries, Javanese became a highly hierarchical language. Linguistic registers, each with its own basic vocabulary, came to mark degrees of formality as well as social deference and difference. Choice of words conveys a sense of the relationship between the speaker and the person addressed. This can be highly nuanced.

Even if they never learn Javanese language, foreign students of gamelan encounter a key aspect of the Javanese articulation of social relationships through speech. Kinship terms are extensively used to address and refer to others. *Mas* (elder brother) is a common term of address for young men, while *Pak* (father) is generally used either for older men or for more distant relationships. The equivalents for women are *Mbak* (elder sister) and *Bu* (mother).

While Javanese is the language of everyday conversation and ceremony, most Javanese also know the national language Indonesian. Stemming from the same linguistic family as Javanese, it shares substantial vocabulary and syntactical resources. It lacks the highly developed hierarchical aspects so central to Javanese, so it is more suited to egalitarian conversation. It was the language of nationalist rebellion against colonial rule and is associated with public life, from schooling to government bureaucracy to politics.

Social deference, related to differences in both status and age, extends beyond word choice to tone of voice and body language in accordance with the principle of appropriate behavior. Speakers will often adopt a soft monotone in speaking to people they consider to be their social superiors; they may even be hesitant to speak at all. They will hold their arms close to their bodies and avoid pointing with the finger, indicating objects and people with their thumb if required. Conversely, people who occupy a superior status in relation to those they address may speak in a louder voice, gesturing more openly, and so on. On the other hand, they may choose to embody a high degree of refinement appropriate to their rank. Extremes of such behavior are modeled for all to see by actors in traditional theater and especially by the shadow puppets in *wayang*. In general, politeness demands that one lower oneself as one passes by seated people, particularly if they are older or of higher status. This is readily apparent when Javanese musicians take their places at the instruments in a gamelan. The more polite and particularly the lower in status will walk half bent over, their right arms extended low to the ground, gently cleaving the space in front of them as they make their way past other musicians. Deeply inculcated patterns of deference also mean that when musicians come to play without predetermined assignments, the leading instruments are likely to remain open while musicians seat themselves at the less prominent instruments, leaving the best places open to others (see Brinner 1995).

Independence. *Even as Javanese performing arts were enjoying their greatest royal support, resistance to the Dutch was taking a new pan-Indonesian form, unlike earlier resistance, such as a localized revolt led by a Javanese prince (1825–1830). Thanks in part to the printing presses and formal education introduced by the Dutch and to new Muslim organizations, Indonesian nationalism spread, laying the groundwork for the future republic but not yet being powerful enough to overthrow the Dutch. It was the Japanese conquest of Indonesia in 1942 that accomplished that. In 1945, at the end of World War II, the Dutch attempted to return even as Indonesians declared independence. The ensuing struggle ended in 1949.*

Gamelan at the Radio Station.   Radio Republik Indonesia Surakarta, known by its acronym RRI, is the main radio station in Solo. It is part of the network of radio stations established by the Indonesian government as soon as independence was declared in 1945. These stations became important organs of state propaganda. They also served to unify musical practice to a considerable extent. This is one impact of mass media on musical life.

As a social and physical environment for gamelan, RRI differs greatly from the courts. The extreme patterns of deference required in the palace are not appropriate here. Instead of a *pendhapa*, RRI has a Western-style auditorium with proscenium stage. The gamelan is arranged in the orchestral pit at the foot of the stage. It differs little from the palace gamelan in size and component instruments. A large staff of musicians is employed full time and plays for various regular programs including listener requests. For some broadcasts, they may read notation from blackboards since some pieces are new and may never be played again. Some of the best musicians in Solo have been on the radio station staff, which was originally built up from musicians who left the royal courts shortly after the establishment of the Republic of Indonesia. Other groups, such as amateur men's or women's groups, also perform at the station; gamelan competitions are held there, too. Since the staff musicians are full-time state employees, they spend a lot of time in the auditorium. If you walked into a rehearsal, you might see the female singers scattered among the auditorium seats, some of them looking at magazines as they sing. For a shadow play performance at the station, on the other hand, they would be on display on the stage above the instrumentalists, dressed in striking colors, hair done up in a large traditional bun, and faces transformed by cosmetics. The atmosphere can get quite rowdy if the shadow master pokes fun at his male musicians or flirts with the female singers (via one of his puppets), evoking catcalls and laughter from musicians and members of the audience.

When the radio station puts on a shadow play, the auditorium often fills up despite the fact that admission is charged and the seats are oriented toward the lit side of the screen rather than the shadows. Many, many more people listen over the airwaves, even though they cannot see the puppets or their shadows. Their knowledge of this art form and the stock characters enables them to imagine the action. At night I would often see pedicab (*becak*) drivers slumped in their vehicles listening to a *wayang* over the radio while they waited for customers.

Reformasi. *Indonesia's early experiment in democracy was aborted first by the strong hand of the first president, Sukarno, and then by years of thinly masked military dictatorship with extensive censorship and squashing of dissent under President Suharto. The overthrow of Suharto in 1998 opened the floodgates for public expression with calls for reformation (reformasi) of corrupt government. It also strengthened threats to the unity of the nation as East Timor succeeded in breaking away and Aceh at the western end of the country intensified its fight to follow suit. Such separatism is not only*

an expression of a desire for local autonomy per se but also a revolt against the Javanese center. The Javanese, the largest ethnic group within Indonesia, have always dominated the Indonesian military and the government, sparking resentment in other parts of the country (see, e.g., Sutton 2002). Unrest has not been limited to the other islands, however, or to resistance against Javanese. Solo came to the fore in 1998 as rioters destroyed or damaged numerous buildings.

Returning to Java in 2000 after an absence of seven years, I learned that many people who formerly would have hired a full gamelan for an occasion were turning to a smaller, more contemporary, cheaper solution. This was the *campursari* (meaning "mixture of essences") mentioned earlier (CD track 3), a genre of popular songs performed on an ensemble that combines electric guitar, bass, and keyboards with a few gamelan instruments (see Supanggah 2003). The sudden popularity of the form gained additional support from economic factors. A steep decline in the value of Indonesian currency followed by the popular revolt against the long-standing authoritarian regime of Suharto brought about a situation in which few could afford to sponsor a full gamelan performance. *Campursari* offered a cost-effective contemporary solution but damaged the livelihood of gamelan musicians who did not choose to play this kind of music. It is too early to say what the long-term effect of this change will be, but recent reports indicate that *campursari* is no longer as popular as it was at the turn of this century.

SIMILARITIES AND DIFFERENCES

If you were to make the rounds of the performances I have just described, you would notice some recurring characteristics. Almost all these events are open to the public, with no admission charged. This does not mean that musicians necessarily play for free; the costs are usually paid by a sponsor such as the city hall, other civic and business organizations, a neighborhood organization, or a private individual. Another common characteristic is that little (if any) advance notice is given. I found this a challenge when planning fieldwork because I rarely learned of a performance more than a few hours in advance. Another common characteristic is that people feel free to come and go. There are no program notes and usually no announcements, but people still know when the end of the performance is approaching. They do not applaud, and when they realize that a typical ending piece is being played, most leave without waiting for the last note to sound. Rarely are there age limitations on audiences: they can include people of all ages, and it is not uncommon to see musicians sitting with a child or grandchild in their lap or leaning on their side or back. However, there are some clear gender differences: some venues and occasions tend to draw almost exclusively male audiences, and instrumentalists in most public performances are almost exclusively male. Class distinctions are far less clear. While many musicians come from relatively poor families, a few are aristocrats, and one can expect to find people of various social backgrounds in the audience. Not all Javanese like or patronize gamelan music, but as a whole it is not associated exclusively with any social class. You would be unlikely to see orthodox Muslims in the audience or as musicians because this segment of Javanese society generally rejects gamelan and its associated theater and dance.

There are also some striking differences from one performance to the next. From the opulence of the Mangkunagaran *pendhapa*, to the auditorium seating of RRI, to the iron gamelan playing in an alley to mark Independence Day, to the itinerant *siter* player busking in the streets, the physical setting, the audience, and the performers contrast strongly. The instruments range from centuries-old bronze heirlooms with the initials of the king carved in their wooden cases to a simple box zither with unraveled bicycle brake cables serving as strings. The demeanor of the audience would be quite different, too, in their behavior toward each other and toward the musicians. The laughter and catcalls at a *wayang* are a far cry from the respectful quiet in one of the palaces, yet some of the same musicians may be present at both locations.

ACTIVITY 1.3 *In a brief essay, contrast the norms of audience and musician behavior at performances of music that you know with what I have described in various contexts in Java. Characterize the degrees of formality/informality in different performance situations that you have experienced. Take into account the placement and behavior of audience and performer, and the presence or absence of boundaries between them. Can you think of ways in which respect is paid to musicians and instruments?*

Despite the enormous differences in the quality of sound and the surroundings, you might hear the same composition in many of these performances. In every instance, excepting *campursari* (CD 3) and *gamelan sekatèn* (CD 6), you would be likely to hear the vocalists singing poetic texts dating back to the eighteenth and nineteenth centuries, perhaps even some fragments from much older sources. But you might not realize that you were hearing the same piece because most Javanese gamelan compositions can be altered in numerous ways and radically transformed in the process. This is indicative of the fundamental flexibility of many of the frameworks for music making. Much of this book will be devoted to introducing these possibilities and the conventions that enable musicians to manipulate raw materials in individual ways.

Here are some of the specific musical characteristics you would be likely to hear no matter what the context and for almost every type of gamelan. Pieces tend to be long: it is not uncommon for several to be strung together so that the musicians perform for 45 minutes, an hour, or more without stopping. In the course of each piece and medley of pieces, there are typical fluctuations in rhythmic flow; for instance, pieces often begin by slowing down and then proceed through several more changes in speed. Musicians tend to end a piece by accelerating and then slowing to the point where the beat is almost lost. Such fluctuations are almost always led and controlled by a drummer. Gongs of various sizes, pitches, and timbres are played in regular patterns of alternation with each other to mark off the main sections and subsections of a piece. The music flows along in several distinct "layers" characterized by different registers and speeds. In other words, a slow-moving melody is heard together with other parts moving two, four, or eight times as fast. The faster parts tend to sound in the middle and high registers while the slower are concentrated in the lower registers. As the speed of the music changes, some of the layers become more prominent while others recede into the background.

CATEGORIES AND CROSS-CULTURAL (MIS)COMMUNICATION

I have been using the word *music* in a cross-culturally universalist manner, without defining its particular meanings relevant to Central Javanese cultural practices and beliefs. Although I will continue to use the term for the sake of convenience, it is imperative to consider how it maps onto the conceptual categories prevalent in Javanese discourse. No Javanese term has equal breadth of connotation. As Lisa Gold has shown for Bali, "music" is a highly context-specific category (2005). The Javanese and Indonesian word *musik* (derived from Dutch *muziek*) covers a broad array of popular and non-Javanese types of music; however, it does not refer to the music of the gamelan. The current term for gamelan music is *karawitan,* which has connotations of smoothness and refinement. But *karawitan* is also limited in scope since it does not usually include the unaccompanied songs, sometimes known collectively as *tembang,* which are closely related to gamelan music. Forms of theater associated with gamelan are usually referred to by genre without an umbrella term. The scope of this book does not permit exploration of all the terminological complications for music, theater, and dance, but you should keep in mind two things. First, numerous Javanese art forms are closely linked to each other yet compartmentalized at the same time. Second, your assumptions about the meanings of the terms *music*, *theater*, and *dance* will not always match Javanese conceptual categories.

CONCLUSION: THREE THEMES

Flexibility of Frameworks and Processes.   In Central Java both the music that people play and the ensemble on which they perform it are flexible constructs that can be augmented, diminished, or otherwise altered according to the situation. A rich institution or individual is likely to own a large gamelan with many beautiful instruments, but you may find that one of the musicians whom you saw playing on such a large beautiful gamelan can also be heard performing alone, singing and accompanying himself on a *siter* and adapting some of the same pieces to the much-reduced resources at his disposal. Some pieces have even been transferred from gamelan to other ensembles that may include instruments such as guitar and ukulele.

When a Javanese musician composes a new piece or learns an old one, he or she does not determine every detail or expect to have others replicate the piece precisely. Musical compositions are frameworks for playing that can be worked out in different ways depending on the context and musicians' desires. Astonishingly little of this music is truly fixed, only to be performed in one way. This does not mean that anything goes—far from it—but a Javanese musician is constantly adapting both to the circumstances at hand and to fellow performers in this essentially collaborative endeavor. Audiences are aware of this at some level and appreciate the smoothness with which musicians work things out.

Musicians learn flexible ways of making music, processes that can be adapted to different contexts. Musicians who accompany theatrical performances are adept at lengthening, shortening, or otherwise altering pieces in accordance with the action. They will play those same compositions differently to accompany dance or as concert music. In this book you will learn some of the ways that musicians transform compositions to create such differences.

This flexibility is directly linked to primarily oral transmission, which involves very limited use of notation, and to the development of distinctive local traditions. Variation is inherent to Javanese music. It is one of the most attractive aspects of this music both for performers and for listeners. While people have their favorite ways of doing things, they appreciate the ways that individual musicians differ from one another.

Appropriateness. A sense of appropriateness underlies the conventions that constitute a culture. Musical choices can generally be explained in terms of what is culturally appropriate, that is, what fits a particular set of conventions or expectations. To pick a trivial example, if a given type of music is conventionally played softly, then adding a very loud drum must be seen as either a sign of ignorance or a desire to flout convention and confound people's expectations. For Central Javanese music, the question of appropriateness is a central consideration both in theory and in practice. In the traditions associated with the royal courts in particular, it is common to hear musicians talk about the appropriateness of a composition, a song text, or a playing style for a given situation. Such judgments are central to maintaining the sense of balance and refinement idealized by many Javanese. Idiomatic performance of each of the instrumental and vocal parts is one instance of this principle, but it is also manifested in other ways. For instance, I. M. Harjito taught me that it is considered appropriate to follow a calm piece with a livelier one, and vice versa. From comments by him and other musicians, I learned that it is appropriate to perform a given piece in certain ways but not in others that do not fit its character. Ethnomusicologist Marc Benamou wrote an entire dissertation on such judgments of the inherent character of pieces.

Interconnectedness. Javanese music is characterized by great variety, a variety that is bound together by myriad connections. These connections fall into three main categories: between music and other arts such as theater, dance, and poetry; between musical repertoires and individual pieces; and between the individual parts played within an ensemble.

Numerous borrowings, imitations, and adaptations within a single art form and between related forms have created a complex set of connections among the many types of music, theater, dance, and poetry. As a result, a dancer's movements may evoke theatrical associations, drumming for *klenèngan* references certain types of dance, and theatrical performances draw music from a variety of sources—to name just a few such connections. The web of connections radiates between these arts and Javanese literature, including well-known poetry from the nineteenth century (and earlier) and large narratives such as the Mahabharata, the Ramayana, and the Panji tales. Intertextuality is pervasive. These connections enable performers to move with ease between most genres, though a few require highly specialized knowledge. They have been fruitful for the creation of new forms through combinations of aspects from several existing ones, and they endow most Javanese with a detailed knowledge base with which to experience performances through a complex frame of reference.

Javanese gamelan performance is characterized by tight integration of the individual parts. A Javanese composer does not usually specify all the details of a piece, leaving the creation of the individual parts to the performers who will be guided by the extensive set of conventions associated with each instrument in the gamelan. Given a basic melody, musicians will rely on their idiomatic knowledge of instrument-specific conventions (the "idiom" of that instrument) to create the strands that make up the rich, dense texture characteristic of Javanese gamelan. Because of this input from many individuals, there is a great deal of variety in the performances of any piece. Yet there are strong connections between the individual parts, and the performances are usually closely related in many ways. Musicians listen to one another, acutely aware of what others are doing and attuned to the cues that come from those playing leading roles. This interaction is the heart of gamelan performance.

Instrumental (and vocal) idioms are closely related to one another, and it is this interconnectedness that enables musicians to master most (sometimes all) of the instruments of the gamelan. Think how that contrasts with Western orchestral musicians who must specialize, usually mastering no more than one or two instruments. This interconnectedness relates to the concept of social harmony (*rukun*), identified as essential to the functioning of Javanese society by James Siegel, among others (1986).

In this chapter you have encountered a variety of ensembles that exemplify Central Javanese gamelan in an array of contexts. A piece played in one of these contexts may be playable in another and yet judged inappropriate there. To take an extreme example, it would be grossly inappropriate to play a special *gamelan sekatèn* piece on a *siter*. Yet most of the pieces played by a large group of palace musicians on the majestic *gamelan sekatèn* in the courtyard of the great mosque are drawn from the same general repertoire as those played on the humble little *siter* by itinerant musicians who wander the streets playing for money. An amateur gamelan group could, in theory, play either sort of composition, but it would be unlikely to tackle the longer, more serious and majestic pieces. This, too, would be considered inappropriate.

A few pages back, I said that gamelan pieces tend to be flexible and adaptable, but that a highly developed sense of appropriateness constrains the ways that musicians utilize this flexibility and a premium is placed on smoothness and refinement. As you read the following chapters, you will learn about many other such judgments that tell us a lot about Javanese culture as it is received, adapted, and transmitted. In so doing, each person develops a sense of what is musically appropriate in a wide variety of situations.

CHAPTER 2

A Sense of Time

Gong. Say it slow and low. The name of the instrument is its sound, so perfect that it passed into European languages from Malay (a close relative of Javanese) shortly after Europeans first came to Southeast Asia. Gongs from Java are highly prized and have been exported to other parts of Indonesia and Europe for centuries.

The deepest, most resonant sound in the gamelan emanates from the big gong, the *gong ageng*. Forged by hand from a disk of bronze by a crew of skilled artisans, it is also the most difficult instrument to manufacture. Slowly heating, hammering, reheating, and hammering again, the gong smiths thin the disk, stretching it ever wider, and then turn the edge inward to create a deep "lip" around the central disk, the diameter of which can be as much as a yard (see figure 2.1). As one man turns the disk with long tongs, others take turns striking in regular alternation. Each man's hammer is tuned to a different note so that the pattern of striking creates a melody, which you can hear on CD track 8 (together with the sounds of a grinder and another hammer in the background). Further forging shapes the surface of the gong so that a sloping "shoulder" surrounds a flat central circle. In the center of that circle, the smiths add a half-dome bulge, a boss. It is this structure that gives the gong its well-defined pitch, unlike flat tam-tams and many Chinese gongs, which have a much less clearly defined pitch because so many frequencies are heard simultaneously. Just as important as the clear pitch and richness of a gong's timbre is the way that its sound gradually decays, alternately swelling and fading in a wave-like pattern. Connoisseurs distinguish particular gongs by the speed of this alternation (called *ombak*, meaning "wave") and how many times it swells before finally fading out.

The largest gongs are often given personal names, painted in Javanese script on the inside of the gongs, and honored with incense and flowers. They are usually suspended from ornately carved poles (see figure 2.2A). You play the gong by striking the boss with a large padded mallet or the fleshy part of your fist. The right touch is required: too soft a blow and the gong barely sounds; too hard and it roars. Some contemporary

FIGURE 2.1 *Gong forging in the smithy of Tentrem Sarwanto. (Photo by Ben Brinner.)*

Javanese musicians have experimented with distorted sounds as well as striking and scraping other parts of the gong, but in traditional gamelan only the boss is struck. Within the context of gamelan performance, the rich, low sound of the gong conveys a sense of completion and arrival, but it can also mark beginnings.

ACTIVITY 2.1   *Listen to CD track 9, which consists of the beginning and ending of "Ladrang Asmaradana," to hear how the gong 1) marks the point of entry for the full gamelan at the end of the introduction to the piece (played here on a bowed fiddle) and 2) gives a sense of resolution at the end of the piece. Compare to CD track 4.*

MAKING AND MARKING MUSICAL TIME:
GONGS AND DRUMS

Time is the primary axis in music. One of the more striking characteristics of Javanese gamelan in comparison to other musical ensembles is the large number of musicians and instruments involved in shaping

FIGURE 2.2A *Gongs of Gamelan Kyai Udan Mas:* Gong ageng, kempul, *and* gong suwukan. *(Photo by Ben Brinner.)*

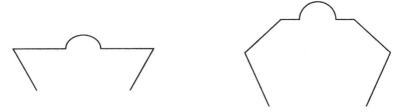

FIGURE 2.2B *Gongs of Gamelan Kyai Udan Mas: Schematic comparison of* kethuk and kenong *cross-sections.*

FIGURE 2.2C *Gongs of Gamelan Kyai Udan Mas:* Kenong *(large kettles) with* kempyang *and* kethuk *(small kettles). (Photo by Ben Brinner.)*

and marking movement along this temporal axis. In a widely cited classification of the instruments of the gamelan, Martopangrawit recognizes two basic subsets (1984): the instruments that cradle the melody and those that cradle the *irama* (a rhythmic concept crucial for understanding Javanese musical time, which I shall explain shortly).

What does Javanese musical time feel like? Most of this music has an underlying pulsation that is very even in character for considerable stretches of time. To the extent that there are regular accents, these occur every 2, 4, 8, or 16 beats. Thus the rhythmic organization is fundamentally binary and the stress is end-weighted (i.e., it falls on the second of two beats, the fourth of four, and so on).

In this chapter you will learn about the various types of gongs that are played to mark off units of time both large and small. Together, the sounds of these gongs interlock in patterns that serve as the temporal frameworks for hundreds of compositions.

You will also learn about drums and basic aspects of drumming. The drummer regulates time, controlling the ensemble's speed, marking progress through a musical form, and creating a sense of excitement, calm, or some intermediate mood. The patterns of sounds played on the drums are closely tied to the colotomic patterns played on the gongs.

Cyclicity and Colotomic Function. In the course of most gamelan pieces, the big gong is heard every time the end of a large section is reached. Because the end of the section is also its beginning, this kind of musical organization in time is called cyclical. It is this cyclicity and its internal organization that Judith Becker compared to calendrical cycles (1979; see chapter 1).

ACTIVITY 2.2 *Listen to CD track 10, "Ketawang Subakastawa," paying particular attention to the big gong. Note the CD time code each time you hear the big gong. How many times do you hear it?*

Cyclicity pervades Javanese music—almost every Javanese piece is based on this organizing principle of recurring sections that lead back to their beginnings. Cycles vary tremendously in duration, from a few seconds to more than eight minutes. There is a corresponding difference in the experience of playing or hearing short and long cycles. The very short ones convey a sense of urgency and excitement, while the long ones generally convey calm. The length of a cycle may also be measured in beats. The common lengths of cycles used in Javanese music are powers of 2: 4, 8, 16, 32, 64, 128, and 256.

Several smaller types of gongs demarcate points within each cycle. Each gong type has its own pitch register and timbre, which the gong smiths create by manipulating the overall size and thickness as well as the proportions of the gong's lip, face, and boss (see figure 2.2B). These different sounds within a gong cycle are like signposts on a path. Since they have a hierarchy of importance, they are also like punctuation, at least in medium and long cycles. The gong is like a period at the end of a sentence, and the smaller gongs act like semicolons and commas. Jaap Kunst, who wrote the first major book on Javanese music, invented the term *colotomic structure* to denote such punctuation. In Martopangrawit's classification, mentioned above, these gongs are said to "cradle" the rhythm.

ACTIVITY 2.3 *Listen to CD track 11. How many different types of gongs do you hear? Do you notice two being played simultaneously?*

The final beat of a cycle is marked by the *gong ageng* for longer cycles. For short cycles a slightly smaller gong, a *gong suwukan*, is often played on the final beat instead because its sound does not last as long, its pitch is a bit higher, and its *ombak* is not as intense. Therefore when the *gong suwukan* is struck frequently due to a short cycle, its sounds do not blur together as the *gong ageng* sounds would.

Within each cycle there are usually two or four parts of equal length, each ending with a stroke on a smaller gong. This is the horizontally suspended *kenong*, which has a much higher pitch than a *gong ageng* as well as different proportions and timbre (see figure 2.2C). A further subdivision of the cycle is played on a smaller, flatter horizontal gong, the *kethuk*. Unlike the *kenong* and gong, which are played at the end of a section, the *kethuk* is played to mark the middle of a unit. This unit ranges from a single beat to 16 beats in length, again in powers of 2. The *kethuk* is usually pitched lower than the *kenong* and has markedly different timbre from all the other gong-type instruments. The *kethuk* player uses a rapid double or triple stroke, damping the *kethuk* with the last stroke. This produces a dull, penetrating thud compared to the bright bell-like sound of the *kenong* or the deep rumble of the *gong ageng*.

Numerous combinations of these three instrumental parts are possible, despite the restrictions already mentioned (cycle length limited to powers of 2 and the hierarchy of *gong ageng, kenong*, and *kethuk*), but Javanese musicians do not use all of them. Over time certain patterns have become established, conventionalized as standard means of organizing music in time.

Some of these colotomic patterns involve two additional instrument types. The *kempul* is a medium-size gong that hangs from a pole, similar to the way large gongs hang and sometimes even sharing the same pole. Its sound lies between the gong and the *kenong* in pitch register and has a warm tone that rapidly gets louder and then softer. Unlike the big gong, it has no *ombak* and it is often damped soon after it is struck. The other commonly played colotomic instrument is the *kempyang*, a small, high-pitched, horizontal gong that looks and sounds like a miniature *kenong*. In those colotomic structures that involve the *kempyang*, this small gong is played before and after each *kethuk* stroke to mark the smallest subdivisions of the cycle. Some gamelans include two or three other instruments that serve as colotomic markers for smaller subdivisions of a cycle, but these are relatively rare and beyond the scope of this book.

ACTIVITY 2.4 *Listen to CD track 12 to hear each of these colotomic gongs played individually, in the following order:* kempyang, kethuk, kempul, kenong, gong suwukan, *and* gong ageng. *Now listen to CD track 11 again and try to identify the different colotomic instruments as they are played.*

The sounds of these gongs are quite distinct, differing not only in register but also in timbre. This is crucial because they provide reference points for musicians in the course of performance. Gamelan musicians know the patterns and are aware of them even when they are playing instruments not involved in marking the colotomic structure. Dancers know them, too, and often depend on colotomic markers to coordinate their choreography with the music.

ACTIVITY 2.5   *Listen again to CD track 11 and follow the* lancaran *pattern notated in figure 2.3. Say the names of the instruments as they are struck, abbreviating* kenong *to "nong,"* kempul *to "pul," and* kethuk *to "tuk" (abbreviations used in the United States; Javanese musicians actually say "tho" and "gung" for* kenong *and* kempul*). Now listen to "Lancaran Singa Nebah Pélog" on CD track 13 and try to hear gong, ke-nong, kempul, and* kethuk *marking the* lancaran *structure in the context of the full ensemble.*

Note that the first two colotomic patterns shown in figure 2.3 are equal in length. Both *lancaran* and *ketawang* have 16-beat cycles, but they differ in the internal subdivision of that cycle. In performance they also are linked to different drum patterns.

ACTIVITY 2.6   *Compare the* ketawang *and* lancaran *co-lotomic patterns notated in figure 2.3. Now listen to the longer* ladrang *pattern on CD track 14 as you follow this notation. Explain how the* ladrang *and* lancaran *patterns differ, and how they are similar. How is the* ladrang *pattern related to the ket-awang pattern?*

The different types of gong vary not only in size, shape, and sound, but also in number and function. A single set includes one *kethuk*, one *kempyang*, and one or two *gong ageng*, however, there may be two or even three *gong suwukan* and as many as seven *kenong* and seven *kempul*. This is because the players of the *kenong* and *kempul* usually match the pitch of the melody note on which they play. Thus, these instruments do more than mark off units of time—they participate in the melody, too. The *kempyang* and *kethuk* not only mark off subdivisions of a cycle but can also impart a feeling of syncopated drive, particularly at a fast tempo.

Lancaran

Kenong	N				N				N				N			
Kethuk	t		t		t		t		t		t		t		t	
Kempul				P				P				P				
Gong																G

Ketawang

Ladrang

Key: • = beat   + = kethuk   = kenong   ( ) = gong   = kempul   = kempyang

FIGURE 2.3 *Sample colotomic patterns.*

32

DRUMMING

Drums and drummers are key to the performance of gamelan in Java. Very few pieces are performed without them. The drummer controls changes of speed and cues the gamelan to start, stop, and shift gears. Of all the players he—there are very few female drummers even in female gamelan groups—is the one who most often "drives" the gamelan, but unlike the conductor of an orchestra, he does not have sole control. All competent Javanese musicians know how to respond to the various cues that the drummer gives. The drummer, in turn, needs to know much more than just how to drum.

The drums most commonly used in Javanese gamelan have two heads of unequal size that are played with hands, not sticks. Usually barrel-shaped, they are carved from a section of tree trunk (preferably jackfruit) with a bulge that is closer to the larger skin, or head. The right hand is the normative hand for playing the larger drum head. However, this norm is often ignored, particularly by village musicians who are less concerned than court and urban musicians with the details of etiquette. So rather than referring to left- and right-hand strokes, I will refer to large and small skins.

The drum (*kendhang*) comes in three main sizes, each with its own name and uses: *kendhang gendhing, ciblon,* and *ketipung* (see figure 2.4). The *kendhang gendhing* is the largest and lowest-pitched; its alternate name, *kendhang ageng* (great drum), refers to this. It is played in a relatively restrained, sparse manner either alone or in conjunction with the smallest drum (*ketipung*), and it is particularly associated with the large-scale compositions called *gendhing*.

Both *kendhang gendhing* and *ciblon* are placed on stands, usually at right angles to each other, one in front of the player and one to his side. Thus when he switches from one to the other in the course of a piece, he rotates 90 degrees. The *ketipung* may also be played on a stand in front of the *kendhang gendhing* but is more often held in the drummer's lap or across one thigh.

The large skin on each *kendhang* is tuned at least a fifth lower than the small one. The drummer will usually tune to the gamelan, but there is considerable room for variation in choice of pitch from one drummer to the next. Drummers regulate the tuning by sliding rings or loops along the V-shaped lacing that connects the two skins. Sliding the tuning ring toward the large skin narrows the V (giving it a Y shape) and tightens both skins. This must be done evenly all around the drum. The tuning can then be further adjusted by tightening one skin or the other with mallet strokes along the rim or by hitting and pushing the center of the skin to loosen it.

FIGURE 2.4 *Drums:* Ciblon, ketipung, kendhang gendhing *in front;* bedhug *in center rear; spare* ciblon *drums standing on end.*

There are two exceptions to these generalizations. First, there are two drums very similar in size to *ketipung* and *ciblon*, but they differ in name, tuning, and function. The more important of these is the *kendhang sabet*, a medium-size drum discussed in chapter 7 on *wayang*. The second exception concerns drums used in certain highly specialized ensembles, principally found at court. Some of these are played in pairs with hard-headed mallets. The largest, the *bedhug*, is played with a padded mallet and is suspended horizontally from a frame not unlike a small gong stand. The *bedhug* (seen without its stand in figure 2.4) is played in *gamelan sekatèn* (you heard its deep thud on CD track 6) and is the only instrument associated with mosques, where it serves to alert the community. In certain dances, it also adds powerful accents to the music and to the dancer's movements. The *bedhug* player, unlike other drummers, does not take a leading role.

A vocabulary of named drum strokes serves as a highly efficient form of oral notation. Knowledge of this drum language is widespread, even among those performers who are not proficient drummers. On CD track 15, you can hear Midiyanto say the names of a few strokes and play them on the medium-size *ciblon*. While the strokes can be written down using letters or other symbols, they are more often recited, either when someone is teaching or when drummers and dancers or puppeteers need to communicate about how a certain part should go. This recitation is often half-spoken, half-sung.

Fundamental to the "language" of Javanese drumming is the contrast between low- and high-pitched strokes. Other strokes, such as slaps and damped strokes, involve "noise" (i.e., their pitch is difficult or impossible to determine).

Another fundamental characteristic of Javanese drumming (particularly on the large and small *kendhang*) is a hierarchy of main strokes and "filler" strokes played between the main strokes. The main strokes are more or less fixed into sequences that are named patterns and may be notated. The filler is less rigidly defined and can be varied considerably without changing the basic identity of the drum pattern.

All three drums share certain basic strokes. Drummers use five main strokes on the *kendhang gendhing* (indicated by uppercase X in figure 2.5). A few other strokes can be played in addition to these main ones (such as *lung*, indicated by lowercase x). The *ketipung*—played only with the *kendhang gendhing*, never alone—has the smallest repertoire of strokes: two main strokes, *dhung* and *tak*, with two softer ones to fill in the beats between the main strokes of the drum pattern. The *ketipung* may be played by the same drummer as the *kendhang gendhing* or by a second drummer. Drumming for many pieces begins and ends on the *kendhang gendhing* (with or without *ketipung*), switching in the middle to *ciblon*. The number of times the drummer switches between drums depends on the piece or medley being performed and can vary greatly.

The most complex drumming is always played by a single drummer on the medium-size *ciblon*. It is also the most flexible, open to numerous alterations and a certain amount of improvisation. The *ciblon* has the largest vocabulary of strokes, and the drummer may add to that by reaching over to the *kendhang gendhing* to play a low-pitched *dhah* for emphasis. Many of the patterns played on *ciblon* are derived from dance drumming and are so closely linked to dance movements that a sort of synaesthesia results—movement and sound are indelibly linked.

name	sign	head struck	playing technique	Gendhing	Ciblon	Ketipung
dhah	ꞁ	large	low-pitched stroke near the edge of the head	X	X	
dhung	ρ	large	higher-pitched stroke in center, partially damping head	X	X	X
lung	ℓ	small	same pitch as *dhung*, but produced by striking the small head while partially damping the large one	x	X	
tak	t	small	slapping the small head while damping the large one	X	X	X
tong	o	small	fingertip striking the rim, producing a complex high sound with a hint of the pitch of the *dhung* stroke	X	X	x
ket	k	large	one or two fingers striking the center while thumb and other fingers rest on the drum head	x	x	x
dang	d	both	*dhah* and *tak* together		X	
dlang	bℓ	both	*dhah* slightly precedes *lang* (an undamped *tak*)		X	

Key: X = main stroke   x = subsidiary stroke

FIGURE 2.5 *Sample of common drum strokes. Note that dhung on the ketipung is actually played with a single finger (or thumb) not far from the rim, about where dhah is played on the larger drums, but it is high in pitch so it is musically equivalent to the dhung on the larger drum. The larger skin on the ketipung is so small that drummers do not actually play a stroke in the middle of that skin.*

36

ACTIVITY 2.7 *Listen to CD track 16 to hear a sequence of* ciblon *patterns (with a melody for reference). Now listen to the same melody on CD track 17 played with a different sequence of drum patterns. Do you hear repetition within each sequence? Which sequence do you think is livelier? Note that the recording, with one microphone on each end of the drum, heightens the separation between the strokes played on large and small heads.*

These two *ciblon* sequences are usually played at the beginning of two consecutive cycles of a *ladrang* or longer colotomic form. They are so common in *klenèngan* that it is nearly impossible to hear a performance without them. Despite this, they actually originated as accompaniment to a type of dance called *gambyong* that was performed by low-class itinerant women but was adapted at the courts in the late nineteenth century to become a mainstay of Javanese presentational dance. The interconnectedness of Javanese performing arts is such that every Javanese musician knows the basic movements associated with these sequences of sounds even if he or she cannot drum or dance.

How are the basic elements of drumming actually put to use? Javanese drumming consists of 1) fixed patterns, which may be filled in but varied only slightly, and 2) more loosely defined drumming, which gives the drummer considerable scope for improvisation. The examples you just heard are of the second variety. I will turn now to the first type.

In principle, each colotomic pattern is associated with its own drum pattern. Generally, a drum pattern is as long as the colotomic pattern with which it is paired. It usually has a variant form for ending the piece. Some musical forms (i.e., colotomic structures) have more than one drum pattern. For instance, numerous drum patterns are appropriate to the 32-beat *ladrang*, probably the most widely performed form. Some will be discussed in subsequent chapters; the focus for now is on drumming for the short *lancaran* form.

Lancaran *Drum Patterns.* The basic drum patterns for pieces in *lancaran* form are played on the pair of *kendhang gendhing* and *ketipung*. You have already heard a very brief example, "Lancaran Singa Nebah Pélog Barang" (CD track 13). It begins, like all other pieces in *lancaran* form, with a melodic introduction played on a single instrument. The drummer joins at a preordained point so that the last *dhung* stroke in his introductory pattern coincides with the gong stroke (hence the final

P of pattern A is circled in figure 2.6). This cues the rest of the musicians to enter at the first gong stroke. In order to ensure that the beat is clear and everyone plays together, the drummer may simply hit a *dhung* on every other beat for the first gong cycle (pattern B in figure 2.6). When the tempo is stable, he switches to the main *lancaran* pattern C. Note that this pattern is congruent with the colotomic pattern both in length and in emphasis since the low *dhah* strokes coincide with the *kempul* strokes.

> **ACTIVITY 2.8**   *Listen to CD track 18 while following figure 2.6. The patterns in figure 2.6 are written with the colotomic parts above them so that you can see how these two ways of regulating musical time fit together. Now try to recite drum pattern C while a friend or classmate recites the colotomic parts. If you have enough people, give each colotomic part to a different person.*

The drummer could, in theory, continue to play this main pattern throughout the piece, but since pieces in *lancaran* form tend to have melodies that span several iterations of the colotomic cycle, there is a larger cycle to be marked every time the end of the melody is reached. To mark this, a variant drum pattern, called *salahan*, is played for the last gong cycle of the melody (pattern D in figure 2.6). Note that the first two *dhah* strokes in the *salahan* do not coincide with the *kempul*, as they do in the main pattern (C). Instead these low stroke accents occur every three beats, creating a cross-rhythm that draws attention to the approaching end of the melody. The cross-rhythm also provides the drummer with a good means of cueing tempo changes.

> **ACTIVITY 2.9**   *Clap a steady beat, stomping your foot on every fourth beat. Now switch to stomping on every third beat, and then back to every fourth. Can you feel how the switch to groups of three grabs your attention? Now, practice saying drum patterns C and D in alternation. First, do so while looking at the symbols in figure 2.6; then try to recite from memory. Finally, recite the drum part together with Midiyanto in the first part of CD track 18 and then with his drumming in the second part of the track. You should do this until you are familiar with the patterns and can associate the syllables with the drum sounds. This aural memory and the mapping of one sound system (drum names) on another (drum sounds) are central to Javanese musical competence.*

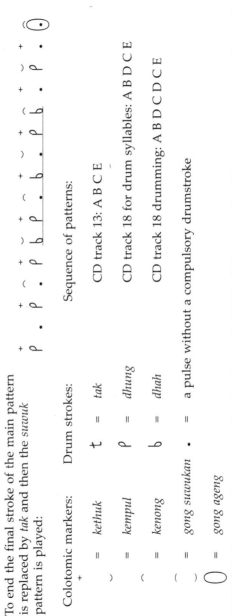

A. Introduction (*buka*)

B. Pattern for first gong cycle, played first time only, substituting for the main pattern C:

C. Main pattern:

D. *Salahan* pattern for the end of the larger melodic cycle:

E. To end the final stroke of the main pattern is replaced by *tak* and then the *suwuk* pattern is played:

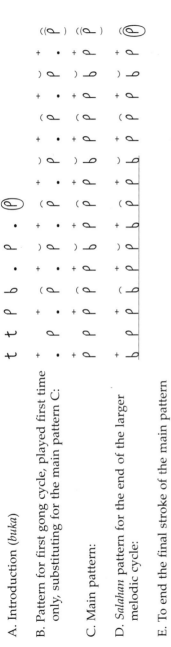

Sequence of patterns:

CD track 13: A B C E

CD track 18 for drum syllables: A B D C E

CD track 18 drumming: A B D C D C E

Colotomic markers:

+ = *kethuk*

) = *kempul*

(= *kenong*

(= *gong suwukan*

) = *gong ageng*

Drum strokes:

t = *tak*

ρ = *dhung*

b = *dhah*

• = a pulse without a compulsory drumstroke

FIGURE 2.6 Lancaran drum patterns with colotomic parts. *Underlining indicates groupings of three that run counter to the overall duple rhythmic organization. On CD track 18 the* salahan *pattern alternates with the main pattern for a lancaran whose melody repeats every two gong cycles. The melody of "Lancaran Singa Nebah" (CD tracks 19 and 26) repeats every three gong cycles so the* salahan *is played for every third cycle.*

39

One pattern in figure 2.6 remains to be explained. This is the pattern that cues the other musicians to slow down and end the *lancaran*. Before he plays this *suwuk* pattern (E in figure 2.6), the drummer accelerates (usually during the *salahan* pattern), and then runs through the piece once or twice more at a faster speed. As the penultimate gong is struck he starts the *suwuk* with a slap on the *ketipung* drum. This stroke, called *tak*, can be played loud enough to cut through the sound of a full gamelan. The *suwuk* pattern that follows is designed to give the drummer control over the ensemble as it slows to a halt.

> **ACTIVITY 2.10** *Write out the* salahan *and* suwuk *patterns, one above the other. How do they differ? What do they have in common?*

Comparison of *salahan* and *suwuk* drum patterns shows that both feature a recurrence of the low *dhah* strokes once every three strokes. There is a larger principle at work here: patterns of three create cross-rhythms relative to the basic duple organization of the colotomic pattern. This stands out and grabs one's attention, so it is useful for endings as it cuts through the texture created on the other instruments.

Pieces in *lancaran* form can have melodies as short as a single colotomic cycle or as long as ten (i.e., 160 beats). The drumming reflects both levels of organization, articulating the individual cycles and the repetition of the overall melody. Both the pattern C and the *salahan* fit the 16-beat cycle common to all pieces in *lancaran* form, but the *salahan* also demarcates the longer cycle of the specific melody. When we recorded CD track 18, I asked Midiyanto to drum as if we were playing a *lancaran* with a melody that lasted for two gong cycles. Therefore, he played the *salahan* pattern every other cycle. By contrast, the melody of "Lancaran Singa Nebah" extends over three gong cycles so the *salahan* is played every third *gongan* (gong cycle) after two iterations of pattern C. The performance on CD track 13 is so abnormally short that the drummer does not play the *salahan* at all, going directly to the *suwuk* at 0:14 and "putting on the brakes" by delaying the low *dhah* strokes. The longer performance of this piece on CD track 19 gives you the opportunity to hear the *salahan* twice, once at 0:19, where drummer uses it to slow the ensemble down drastically, and again at 3:12, where he uses the same pattern to accelerate.

What happened between these two points? A *lancaran* may be repeated with only slight fluctuations in tempo. In CD track 19, however, the drummer cues much more extreme changes. This sets in motion a process ubiquitous in Javanese music that has few parallels elsewhere in the world. The tempo can be halved (roughly), leading to an approximate doubling of the length of each beat and the gong cycle. This is a change in *irama*.

As the beat is stretched to twice its prior duration, there is more time to fill in, so the drum part changes, as do other parts in the ensemble. Instead of one drum stroke for every beat, there are now two (see figure 2.7 for a graphic representation of the increasing ratio between the main beat and the parts that fill in; the elaborating instruments noted in the table will be discussed in the next chapter). Notice that the drummer does not complete the *salahan* that he starts at 0:19, altering its end (at 0:24) to fill in the beats that have now stretched to become twice as long. From this point on, he switches to a drum pattern that is appropriate to the more expansive *irama*, returning to the drumming you have learned only when he returns to the original tempo and *irama* at 3:04.

Pieces in *lancaran* form usually start at a very fast pace, true to their name—*lancaran* means flowing. This initial tempo, and the relationship between the beat and the faster parts, is called *irama lancar*. When the tempo is halved and the beat doubles in length, the new relationship is called *irama tanggung* (hereafter *irama* 1). It is possible to halve the tempo and double the length of the beat again to reach *irama dadi* (hereafter *irama* 2), as the musicians do on CD track 19. This is the most expansive *irama* used for pieces in *lancaran* form. Pieces in longer forms can be expanded even further, to *irama* 3 (*wiled*) and once again to *irama* 4 (*rangkep*), yielding five different *irama* levels in all (see figure 2.7). To experience a greatly expanded *irama* listen again to CD tracks 16 and 17 where nearly 4 seconds elapse between one melody note and the next, while the *ciblon* drumming fills in the space between the beats.

A drummer can also accelerate from a relatively expansive *irama* to a more condensed one. Just as when slowing down, the drummer starts to change speed during a gong cycle and switches patterns as the cycle nears its end.

You probably noticed that the melody of "Lancaran Singa Nebah" changes, too. With each expansion it doubles and when the *irama* is condensed the melody reverts to its more condensed form, a transformation that will be analyzed in chapter 3. Although you have not yet learned to read Javanese notation, you can see these relationships in figure 2.8 by comparing the main melody—represented by numbers—with the colotomic parts, represented by the symbols that you learned to read in this chapter.

Irama Level	Irama Name	Ratio of Main Beat to Fastest Pulse	Top: *Bonang Panerus, Gambang, & Siter* Middle: *Saron Peking, Bonang Barung, & Gendèr* Bottom: Main or Conceptual Beat
1/2	*lancar*	1:2	(beat pattern)
1	*tanggung*	1:4	(beat pattern)
2	*dados*	1:8	(beat pattern)
3	*wiled*	1:16	(beat pattern)

FIGURE 2.7 Irama in Javanese gamelan music. The main beat is often, but not always, manifest in the saron (metallophone) melody. Irama rangkep, also known as irama 4, is not shown here but can be deduced from irama 3 by doubling the pattern. The ratio of the main beat to the fastest pulse is 1:32. Note that Javanese music theorists refer to the five levels of irama in terms of the ratio between the main beat and the gendèr barung rather than the fastest pulse, i.e., 1:1, 1:2, 1:4, 1:8, and 1:16.

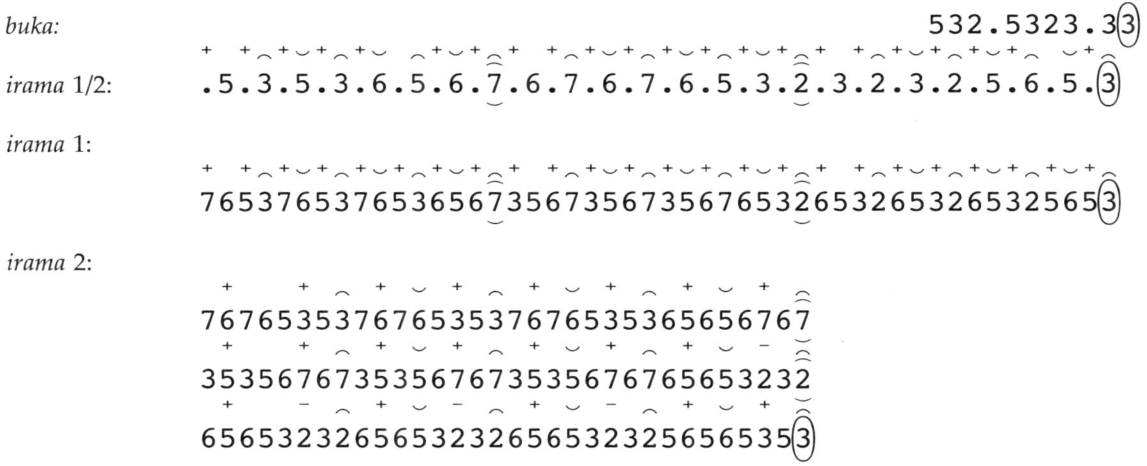

buka:

532.5323.3③

irama 1/2:

```
 +   +  +  +  +   +  (  +  )   (  +  )  +  (  +  )  +  (  +  )  +  ((  +   +  (  +  )  +  (  +  )  +   )  +
.5 . 3 . 5 . 3 . 6 . 5 . 6 . 7 . 6 . 7 . 6 . 5 . 3 . 2 . 3 . 2 . 5 . 6 . 5 . ③
```

irama 1:

```
 +    +  (  +  )  +  (  +  )  +   ((  +    +  (  +  )  +  (  +  )  +   ((  +    +  (  +  )  +  (  +  )  +
7 6 5 3 7 6 5 3 6 5 6 7 3 5 6 7 3 5 6 7 6 5 3 2 6 5 3 2 6 5 3 2 5 6 5③
```

irama 2:

```
 +     +  (  +  )  +  (  +  )  +   +    +  (  +  )  +  (  +  )  +   +    ((
7 6 7 6 5 3 5 3 7 6 5 3 5 3 7 6 5 3 5 3 6 5 6 5 6 7 6 7
 +     +  (  +  )  +  (  +  )  +   +    +  (  +  )  )  ((
3 5 3 5 6 7 6 7 3 5 3 5 3 5 6 7 6 7 6 5 6 5 3 2 3 2
 +     -  (  +  )  -  (  +  )  +   -    +
6 5 6 5 3 2 6 5 6 5 3 2 3 2 6 5 6 5 6 5 3 5③
```

FIGURE 2.8 *"Lancaran Singa Nebah Pélog" in expanded irama showing colotomic parts and melody.*

> **ACTIVITY 2.11**　*Listen to CD track 19, noting each change of irama. The musicians begin to slow from irama lancar to irama 1 at 0:19. When do they slow further to irama 2? What is the time code when they begin to accelerate? The musicians reach irama 1 at 2:54. What is the time code when they reach irama lancar? Even though you do not yet know all the instruments, try to characterize the changes in musical texture that occur when the irama changes.*

A *lancaran* may also be played with more complex and variable drum patterns on the *ciblon*. This is particularly common in dance accompaniment. You can hear an example of this on CD track 20, where the drummer begins drumming on the *ciblon* at 0:13 after playing pattern C (see figure 2.6) only once.

GONGS, DRUMS, AND THE FLEXIBILITY OF TIME

Pieces in *lancaran* form offer a first entry into Javanese musical time as it is demarcated and energized by gongs and drums. Other colotomic forms and drum patterns are longer and more complex but exhibit many of the principles you have just encountered.

Most Javanese pieces are composed to fit conventional colotomic patterns. Each of these has one or more drumming patterns associated with it, and those patterns are congruent in length with the colotomic cycle. Drum patterns are differentiated by the following characteristics: duration, sequence of strokes, and type of drum. Sometimes the drum accents coincide with colotomic accents, but this is not always so. In fact, the drum parts for the longest forms sometimes avoid the strongest beats altogether. This seeming paradox actually makes sense if you consider the refinement that characterizes the pieces in these longest forms. Note how different the role of the drum in Javanese music is from musical systems that do not have colotomic patterns where the drums often create the groove and delineate all the important accents.

Changes in drum pattern transform the music. They cue the musicians to end a piece, expand or contract it (i.e., change *irama*), or go on to another section. As you saw in "Lancaran Singa Nebah" these transitions take place within the cycle, not at its end.

Javanese colotomic forms may at first appear rigid. Certainly their representations on paper can give that impression. But they are malleable, flexible sets of relationships in time, which the musicians can stretch and compress under the guidance of the drummer and in accordance with the situation. Various nuances are vital to this musical practice but difficult to represent on paper. One of these could be called colotomic nonsynchrony: while the notation implies that the colotomic instruments are struck precisely on the beat, slightly delayed strokes of the larger ones—the gong, *kenong*, and *kempul*—are considered more appropriate in many circumstances. This makes these parts stand out and gives the music a looser, more laid-back feeling. Another type of looseness is apparent at the end of a cycle (in longer pieces) and at the end of a piece when time is stretched, each beat taking a bit longer than the one before it. At such moments the drummer does not reinforce a rigid temporal matrix but guides musicians in reshaping musical time. You can hear this at the end of CD track 9, for instance.

Carefully regulated fluctuations in speed are key to the performance practice of Javanese gamelan. Almost every performance of a piece will include several changes. The more moderate changes remain within one *irama*, while greater changes in speed, roughly doubling or halving the duration of the beat, cause changes in *irama*. Here the beat changes, but the fastest pulse—what ethnomusicologist Mantle Hood dubbed the "density referent"—bounces back to about the same rate. In other words, after a shift in *irama*, the fastest parts will be moving at roughly the same rate they were moving before the *irama* change. However, the relationship between their pulse and the conceptual beat

ACTIVITY 2.12   *Listen again to the changes in speed toward the end of "Lancaran Singa Nebah (CD track 19)." Now follow the changes in speed in the "Talu," a medley of pieces played at the beginning of a shadow play (CD track 21). Write down the time code for each change. Try to guess whether there was a change of* irama *or only a change of tempo. What is the overall trend in this sequence?*

will have changed by a factor of two (see figure 2.7). I said "about the same rate" because in fact the pulse in *irama* 2 is usually somewhat slower than that in *irama* 3. This, in turn, is slower than the pulse in *irama* 4, the most expansive *irama* in which the faster parts in the gamelan are moving along at breakneck speed while others progress at a glacial pace.

Changes in tempo and *irama* serve to breathe life into this music. When coupled with changes in loudness, they can be quite dramatic in effect. Extreme examples of such reinforcement are stylistic innovations of the last decades of the twentieth century.

A drummer must master numerous patterns and also develop flexibility in application of these patterns in ways that are appropriate to the different interconnected circumstances of performance. The drummer must also know the limits of the tempo within a given *irama*: the tempo can fluctuate within each *irama*, but should it slow to roughly half its previous value or speed up to double that value, a change of *irama* is triggered and the relationship between the faster gamelan instruments and the basic beat doubles or halves as well. In turn, musicians develop flexibility in order to respond appropriately to the drummer, knowing whether he is simply accelerating a bit—perhaps to announce the approaching end of the piece—or is cueing a change of *irama*.

The themes of flexibility, appropriateness, and interconnnectedness all apply here. There is scope for variation in tempo, but the drummer should consider what is appropriate to the performance context and the particular piece. For instance, the tempo of *irama* 2 in shadow play performances can be considerably faster or slower than in *klenèngan*, depending on the dramatic context. Thus, musicians must maintain a flexible sense of the pace of a piece. In *klenèngan* some pieces are considered more serious, serene, or regal, necessitating a slower tempo, while a lively tempo is deemed appropriate for other pieces. In any case, the drummer must be aware of the fastest instrumental parts in order to set a tempo that is neither impossibly fast nor so slow that the musicians think they should double the speed of their parts to fill in the "spaces" between the beats.

Knowing what is appropriate for a given musical situation (including the constraints of accompanying dance or theater) is a key element in a musician's competence. This in turn highlights the numerous interconnections that link every aspect of Javanese gamelan to numerous others. The choice of tempo is linked to performance context, as is the choice of drums and drumming style. The slight delays with which good musicians play *kenong* and gong are also fine examples of both the flexibility and the sense of appropriateness that pervade Javanese gamelan. These aspects of rhythmic organization serve as a framework for and respond to the melody, subject of the next chapter.

CHAPTER 3

Gamelan, Tuning, and Instrumental Melody

The first thing that strikes most people when they encounter a Javanese gamelan is the sheer quantity of metal and carved wood. Round gongs, ranging in diameter from a few inches to three feet, hang vertically in rows from wooden stands or rest horizontally on thin ropes stretched across wooden frames. Most of the other instruments have rows of keys, more or less rectangular in shape but varying in size. If the gongs and keys are newly forged bronze or have recently been polished, they sport a brilliant golden sheen. If they are old and left to develop a patina, their surface is more subtle, a rich motley golden-green. Cheaper instruments made of iron, often salvaged from truck suspensions and other scrap metal, may be painted to emulate this color. In any case, the wooden cases are likely to be carved in floral patterns and painted in green, brown, or red with gold leaf highlights. Fancier sets are ornately carved with images such as a mythical serpent king carved along the top of the gong stand (see Quigley 1996 and Vetter n.d. for photos of fantastic and highly unusual examples). A gamelan of good quality is an expensive item that serves as a symbol of prestige. Its value increases with time as the bronze ages and settles in molecular structure and (as a result) timbre and tuning. Spiritual power may also be ascribed to it. No wonder that each of the Javanese courts owns several gamelans and that kings restricted the ownership of a full gamelan in former times (see Vetter n.d. for full information on Yogyakarta palace gamelan).

When I first arrived in Java, I borrowed a *gendèr* (a metallophone) from the music academy and bought a *rebab* (a bowed lute; see figure 3.1) from a stall in the market outside the Mangkunagaran palace. The stall had music supplies such as mallets and cord for hanging gongs, as well as flutes and a few brass gamelan instruments of questionable quality. For bronze instruments, you could not simply go to a store and choose from various brands as you might buy a guitar or piano. Since most Javanese musicians do not own their own instruments but use sets belonging to a wealthy patron or an institution, one rarely buys a used instrument from a musician. Occasionally one can find somebody selling a gamelan (either as a set or piecemeal), but most instruments are made to order by a gong smith and his network of craftsmen who specialize in elements such as drums or carved wooden frames and racks.

An American acquaintance ordering supplementary instruments for a gamelan in the United States took me to Pak Tentrem Sarwanto, a young gamelan maker who had taken up the family business with his brothers and some other men (see figure 2.1); I know of no female gong smiths. At that time his business was still small, but it has prospered greatly since then thanks to numerous orders from foreign students and from institutions in Indonesia and abroad.

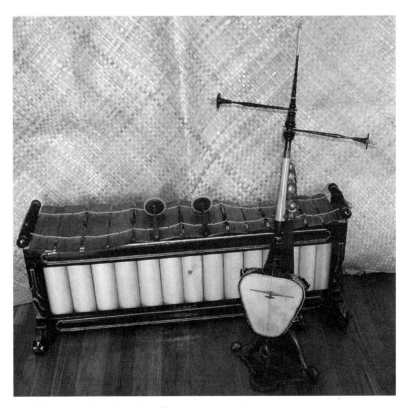

FIGURE 3.1 Rebab *and* gendèr. *(Photo by Ben Brinner.)*

The tools Pak Tentrem had inherited included hammers of many shapes and sizes, specialized for different stages in the forging of bronze gongs and keys. There were stones with rounded hollows (against which the bosses of gongs could be shaped), and numerous tools. Outside the forge stood stacks of crucibles for melting different quantities of metals to create the right alloy of tin, copper, and traces of other metals (see figure 3.2). There also were clay molds for casting the roughly shaped disks and bars that would then be forged into gongs and keys. The building in which the forge was located was kept fairly dark so that the smith could judge the heat of the metal. A pit full of

FIGURE 3.2 *Crucibles and hammers for forging gamelan instruments at the gong smithy of Tentrem Sarwanto. (Photo by Ben Brinner.)*

coal, fired by hand-pumped bellows, was used to heat the metal; a pool of water was used to quickly cool the newly forged instruments.

The process for forging keys for metallophones is simpler than the complex gong forging described in the previous chapter. The component metals are melted, mixed together, and then poured into the appropriate mold, just as they are for gongs. One man hammers the resulting bar while another holds it with long tongs and periodically reheats it (see figure 3.3). After a few strokes, it must be heated again. Once the bar has achieved the desired shape, it is cooled in water and then filed, sanded, and polished. Two holes are drilled in order to suspend the key over its resonator. Tuning is accomplished by scraping or filing away the underside of the key—lowering the pitch by taking from its middle or raising it by filing near the ends (see Quigley in Resources under the Viewing section (1989).

Forging bronze gongs and keys is difficult, intensive hand labor that requires great skill and knowledge. One stroke of the hammer in the wrong place can ruin days of work, though all is not lost as it would be with a choice piece of wood carved for a violin, for instance, since the misshapen

FIGURE 3.3 *Forging a bronze key, gong smithy of Tentrem Sarwanto. (Photo by Ben Brinner.)*

bronze can be melted down and forged again. Gong smithing is a hereditary craft that traditionally has been considered to be spiritually charged and dangerous, requiring offerings to protect the smiths. The cheaper iron instruments are easier to make because the metal is cut to size from manufactured sheets and hammered cold rather than melted, molded, and forged. The manufacture of drums, flutes, and carved wooden cases is somewhat less skilled and not spiritually fraught.

GAMELAN TUNINGS

In theory, no two gamelan sound exactly alike, due partly to the complexities of hand forging but mainly to tuning decisions. There is no standard tuning in Central Java. There is no standard for the relative sizes of the intervals; overall, some gamelans are tuned higher than others, though the differences are not huge. Theorists (mainly non-Indonesian ones) have attempted to establish normative tunings and mathematical models, but they fail to explain the varied abundance of tunings.

Because of the uniqueness of tunings, the instruments in each set are tuned to sound right with one another. Aside from easily tunable instruments such as drums and string instruments (*rebab* and *siter*), the instruments of different gamelan are not interchangeable. Even if a musician does own a *gendèr*, for instance, there is no point in bringing it to a performance because it is unlikely to match the tuning of the other instruments.

In actual practice, some gamelans are tuned alike because a person can ask to have one set tuned to match another. Pak Tentrem suggested matching my new instruments to the gamelan at the radio station. As this gamelan was heard not only on broadcasts but on numerous cassettes, I agreed. This made it much easier for me to play along with cassettes as I was learning. Over time the tuning of my instruments changed as newly forged bronze always does. Pak Tentrem retuned them twice, not in reference to the radio gamelan any more but to make them sound good as a set.

This brings up another aspect of tuning: Making the instruments sound right as an ensemble does not necessarily mean matching all the pitches precisely. Many gamelan tuners (who may or may not be gong smiths as well) purposefully "stretch" octaves, tuning the higher instruments a bit sharp and the lower ones a bit flat, because they feel that the ensemble sounds best that way. This can give a hint of the shimmer achieved in Balinese ensembles by paired tuning (see Gold 2005). All of these variables contribute to the individual character of a gamelan that is recognized and appreciated by musicians much as a wine connoisseur knows wines.

TUNING SYSTEMS: *SLÉNDRO* AND *PÉLOG*

Tuning variability is constrained by two categories or systems named *pélog* and *sléndro*. *Pélog* consists of seven pitches (numbered 1 through 7 in Javanese notation), while *sléndro* has five (numbered 1, 2, 3, 5, and 6; the 4 is omitted because of equivalences between the two systems explained below). This numbering system is the common Javanese method of notation called *kepatihan*. Named after the residence of the king's minister (*patih*) in which it was invented, this notation system was the only notation system to gain wide acceptance, though several others were developed in Java in the late nineteenth and early twentieth centuries. It is relatively straightforward, using horizontal lines above the numbers to join together notes that subdivide a single beat (an idea borrowed from the beams of staff notation) and letters or auxiliary signs to indicate colotomic markers. You have already encountered this system in figures 2.6 and 2.8.

While the "spacing" of these pitches (i.e., the intervals between them) varies from one set of instruments to the next, it is not random, and there is enough difference between the two systems that they remain distinct. In other words, there are two perceptual categories named *sléndro* and *pélog*, and the instruments in a gamelan are tuned to either one or the other. Thus a complete Central Javanese gamelan consists, in essence, of two sets of instruments, one in each tuning system. A few instruments, such as the drums and biggest gongs, do double duty, played for either tuning system. Single gamelan sets exist, too, tuned either to *pélog* or to *sléndro*.

ACTIVITY 3.1 *Listen to the pitches of* sléndro *and* pélog *played in ascending and descending order on a large metallophone from the University of California (UC) at Berkeley's Gamelan Kyai Udan Mas (CD track 22). This is followed by two pentatonic subsets of* pélog: *first pitches 12356, then 23567. On CD track 23, you will hear the introduction to "Lancaran Singa Nebah" played first in* pélog *and then twice in* sléndro *in two differently tuned gamelan. On CD track 24, these same tunings are compared with the closest pitches in Western equal temperament (the synthesized tones). Refer back to CD track 3 to hear the clash between the* pélog *tuning of the gamelan and the diatonic scales played on the synthesizer and guitars in* campursari.

With so much flexibility in tuning, one can become disoriented. At a radio broadcast of an amateur group that had invited me to play *gendèr*, a singer asked me to go over a melody with him during the break between pieces. It was fortunate that we did practice because the pitch he chose by pointing to a key on the *gendèr* proved to be wrong. Although he sang the entire song quite nicely, adjusting to the intervals on the *gendèr*, he ended his solo one note too high. Since this was to serve as the introduction to a piece performed by the entire ensemble, it would have been disastrous to have the musicians enter on the "wrong" note. Aware of such dangers, the *dhalangs* (shadow masters) whom I interviewed repeatedly cited the importance of hearing reference pitches from the gamelan so that they could start their songs on the right pitch and sing in tune with the gamelan. This was particularly crucial when they were performing far from home, using a gamelan provided by the host.

There is yet one more variable to consider to complete this schematic understanding of a gamelan's tuning. This is the relationship between the two tunings. If the two halves of the gamelan have been made as a complete set, they will have at least one pitch in common. Often this is pitch 6 or 5, but it can also be 1 or 2—see figure 3.4 for two possible alignments of the two tuning systems. I have not specified interval sizes because these may vary slightly even within one gamelan, but the spacing of the numbers should give you an idea of the relative size of intervals within and between tuning systems.

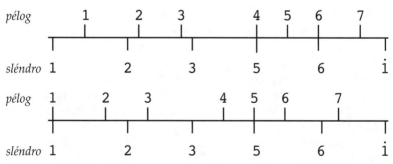

FIGURE 3.4 *Two possible correspondences between* pélog *and* sléndro *tunings of a gamelan.*

GAMELAN INSTRUMENTS

It is time to introduce the rest of the instruments and to learn about their basic construction and ranges. Figure 3.5 shows the instruments of Kyai Udan Mas, the gamelan at UC Berkeley on which some of the CD examples were recorded. Figure 3.6 shows the instrument ranges based on the *sléndro* instruments of that gamelan. These examples cannot be fully representative because gamelan can vary greatly in number, type, and quality of instruments.

ACTIVITY 3.2 *Several gamelan performance groups in North America and Europe have websites that feature photos of their instruments. Find three of these (try the American Gamelan Institute site in the Resources section) and compare the appearance of their instruments (color, carving, size) and their instrumentation (e.g., how many gongs and sarons).*

Most of the instruments in a gamelan are idiophones—metal gongs or keys are the primary sounding elements. You have already been introduced to the gongs of the gamelan, and several other instruments have been mentioned in passing. A gamelan may have only one *gong ageng*, but it is quite common to have two. They are usually tuned a "step" or two apart. (Since Javanese intervals are flexible in size, I use the term *step* to indicate the interval from one note to the next degree of the scale above or below it.) Their pitch is so low that they match both *pélog* and *sléndro*. The somewhat smaller *gong suwukan* (which sometimes also serve both tunings) vary in number from one to three per tuning. As you can see in figure 3.6, the scale started by the *gong suwukan* is continued by the *kempul*, but since the two instrument types fulfill different colotomic functions, they are considered separate instruments (though often played by the same musician). A set of *kenong* is tuned to the octave above the *kempul*.

One gong-based instrument has not been mentioned so far because it is chiefly used melodically rather than for colotomic parts. It consists of 10 or 12 small gongs suspended horizontally in two rows in low wooden racks (such instruments are called gong chimes in ethnomusicological literature). Two sizes are common: the larger *bonang barung* (referred to hereafter simply as *bonang*) and the *bonang panerus*.

Keyed metallophones are represented in abundance in a full gamelan. One type, the *saron*, has thick keys lying across a trough carved out of

	Saron demung	Set of kenong, kethuk, & kempyang	Various gongs and kempul
	Saron demung		
	Saron demung	Slenthem x 2	Kendhang (Various)
Saron			
		Bonang x 2 & bonang panerus x 2	Gendèr x 3
Saron	Gendèr panerus x 3		
Siter	Rebab	Gambang x 2	

FIGURE 3.5 *Javanese gamelan with instrument names relative to position in photo. The instruments of Gamelan Kyahi Udan Mas, made in the early twentieth century, were donated by Sam and Louise Scripps to the University of California at Berkeley after use at the Center for World Music in the early 1970s.* (Photo by Ben Brinner.)

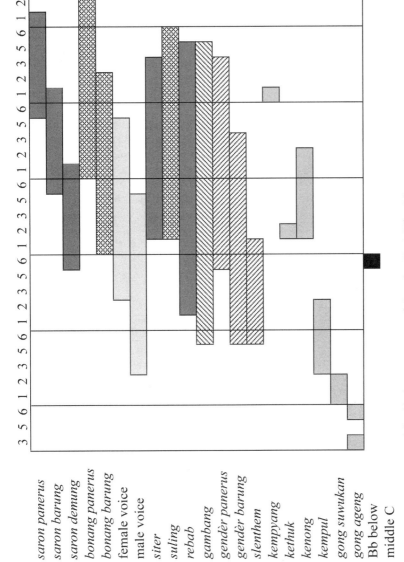

FIGURE 3.6 *Ranges of the sléndro instruments of Gamelan Kyai Udan Mas.*

a large piece of wood that serves as both support and resonator for the keys. It is made in three sizes, ranging from the large *demung* (on which CD track 22 was recorded) to the *saron barung* to the *saron panerus* (also called *peking*). A gamelan will often include one or two of each size; really large ensembles might have four of the medium and large *saron* for each tuning. They are played with relatively hard mallets, made of water buffalo horn for the *peking* and wood for the others. This gives a sharp attack, though the instrument can also be played delicately. Usually a *saron* has seven keys whether it is tuned to *pélog* or *sléndro*. In the latter case, the two "extra" keys extend the range of the instrument beyond an octave (cf. CD track 22). The medium *sléndro saron* also comes in a larger nine-key version on which a musician can improvise elaborations for *wayang*.

The second type of keyed metallophone has much thinner keys suspended by cords over individually tuned resonating tubes. The three variants are the 7-keyed *slenthem*, played with a single mallet, and the 12 to 14-keyed *gendèr barung* (see figure 3.1) and *gendèr panerus*, both of which are played two-handed with two mallets. These mallets are padded, so the resulting sound is radically different from that of the *saron*: It is mellow, with a soft attack and long sustain, unlike the *saron*'s brighter sound, sharp attack, and relatively rapid decay (i.e., quick drop in volume).

While some of the old ceremonial ensembles consist only of metal idiophones and a drum or two, the more common ensembles include several other instrument types: the *gambang* (xylophone), the chordophones *siter* (plucked zither) and *rebab* (bowed spike lute), and an aerophone, the *suling* (end-blown fipple flute). Rounding out the ensemble are the various sizes of membranophone (the *kendhang* introduced in chapter 2) and the singers.

> ACTIVITY 3.3 *Listen to CD track 25 to hear many of these instruments in relative isolation. Certain parts of the ensemble sound throughout this track: the female voice, drums,* slenthem, *and colotomic instruments (you should be able to hear* kempyang, kethuk, kempul, kenong, *and* gong ageng*). Others are featured in the following order:* gendèr, gambang, siter, rebab, *and a pair of* bonang. *Try to match them with the preceding descriptions, and pick them out in the sound of the full ensemble that ends this track. You would not hear such solos in normal performance.*

Numerous conventions shape specific ways in which all these resources for sound production are brought into play together. A few of these conventions were introduced in the previous chapter: the colotomic patterns played out on the gongs, the musical forms delineated by the colotomic patterns, the corresponding drum patterns, and the concept of *irama* (which regulates the rhythmic relationships within the ensemble). Many of the other conventions concern melody.

INSTRUMENTAL MELODY

Melody in gamelan music varies between two radically different performance conceptions: the melodic nuances and free rhythms of unaccompanied song, and the strictly regulated time-delineating rhythms of gong and drum ensembles. Scholars have theorized that the modern gamelan, variable as it is in composition, only came together in the last two centuries, developing out of the confluence of loud ensembles with a preponderance of gongs and soft ones that featured singing, *rebab*, and other soft melodic instruments.

At one extreme, some gamelan music is almost completely devoid of melody. Moments of great tension in theater and dance are often accompanied by *gangsaran*, a form in which the *saron* players repeatedly strike a single note, while the sounds of the various gongs outline a short colotomic pattern similar to *lancaran* and the drummer plays patterns that heighten the intensity and emphasize the movements of the dancers or puppets. The only "melody" you might hear in a *gangsaran* is the brief pattern repeated on the *bonang*, but that is considered an elaboration on the single pitch reiterated by all the other musicians. The contrast between the eerie, insistent monotone of *gangsaran* and the melody of most other gamelan music is extreme. This is why the transition to or from *gangsaran* is so effective in a dramatic context (CD track 20 moves from *lancaran* to *gangsaran* at 0:34 and to a *ladrang* at 1:28).

The Javanese word *lagu*, meaning melody, tune, or song, applies to both instrumental performance and singing. Most of the music played on gamelan features considerable melodic variety, and most of the musicians are engaged in playing or singing melodies. Within the sound world of traditional Javanese gamelan music, there are numerous constraints on *lagu*; at the same time, there is tremendous flexibility.

Among the most basic constraints is the *laras*, the tuning system. A melody will be sung and played either in *pélog* or in *sléndro*, but usually not in both at the same time. Musicians commonly "translate" pieces from *sléndro* to *pélog* (the reverse is rare) or transpose melodies to start on a different pitch within the same tuning. These are prime examples of the principle of flexibility, which permeates Javanese musicality. Perhaps less obvious, but far more fundamental to Javanese musicianship, is the flexibility required to hear a melody as "the same" when it is played on differently tuned gamelans. Recall that there is no standard tuning; for example, not only is *pélog* pitch 5, for instance, not tied to a particular frequency, but the intervals between 5 and its neighbors 4 and 6 can vary considerably in size. The same holds true for all the other pitches and the intervals between them.

Several other factors shape Javanese gamelan melodies. *Pathet*, a term that can be loosely translated as mode, is one of the most challenging concepts in Javanese musical practice and theory and will be discussed briefly in later chapters. Structure, whether colotomic or poetic, is a third constraint on melody. Almost all instrumental melodies are made to fit the symmetrical phrasing of a colotomic structure. Vocal melodies and the instrumental melodies that derive from them are constrained by poetic concerns, which will be discussed in the next chapter. Yet another constraint on melody is idiomaticity. A particular way of making melodies is associated with each instrument, as noted earlier. A vocal melody is rarely similar to a *gambang* melody, for instance, which differs, in turn, from a *gendèr* melody. You can get a sense of some of those differences by listening again to CD track 25.

So how does a Javanese musician conceptualize melody? The first answer might be that there is no prototypical "Javanese musician." Researchers have found considerable individual differences in conceptualization (see Perlman 2004). No standard interpretation holds sway, but in keeping with Javanese philosophy that privileges inner essence over outer form, several Javanese musicians have theorized that the "real" melody of a piece is not performed by any member of the ensemble. Rather, it is revealed in various ways simultaneously by each of them.

Another answer would be that this conceptualization depends on the circumstances: the instrument played, the *irama*, the performance context, and so on. Nonetheless, musicians' melodic conceptualizations must overlap considerably to enable them to make music together and to transfer their knowledge from one set of instruments to another with little (if any) apparent discomfort. This is yet another instance of the extensive interconnectedness of this musical practice. Two significant factors identified by Judith Becker (1980) are central to these shared conceptions—goal tones and melodic contour.

A goal-oriented approach to melody is prevalent among musicians and evident in performance practice. In any piece certain notes serve as the goals for all the various strands in the musical texture. Such notes are called *sèlèh*. They are not the same as the tonal goals in much Western music and are not reached in the same manner. Although certain Javanese musicians adopted a few terms from European music theory, notably tonic and dominant, the precise meanings of the terms did not carry over to Javanese music. Despite the fact that theorists designate a particular pitch as the tonic of a given *pathet* (mode), many of the pieces in that *pathet* will focus and end on other pitches. Notice, for instance, that the pitch labeled 1 is not necessarily more important than any of the other pitches—it is usually not the tonic. "Lancaran Singa Nebah" in *pélog* begins on pitch 3 and usually ends there, too (though it does not have to). However, in the course of its melody, which stretches over three gong cycles, both pitch 7 and pitch 2 become important goals as they coincide with the gong stroke at the end of a cycle.

Placement of a note within the colotomic cycle is one of the main determinants of its importance: By definition, the note that coincides with the gong at the end of a cycle is the most important *sèlèh* within that cycle. Musicians conceive of melodic patterns in terms of their final pitch, their *sèlèh*. They generally learn to play the more elaborate parts by mastering a group of patterns that end on each pitch and then applying these as needed to the *sèlèh* in a given composition.

Contour is another crucial aspect of melodic conceptualization. In a number of publications, Judith Becker pointed to the key role of melodic contour in Javanese music. The way the melody moves from one pitch to another is far more important than absolute interval sizes, especially in view of the highly variable tunings. Figure 3.7A is a graph of the mallet motions required to play the basic *saron* melody of "Lancaran Singa Nebah" in *pélog* and in *sléndro*. Read it from top to bottom, imagining that each column represents a key on a *saron*. From this perspective, melodic contour is a series of motions to the left and right as you move the mallet to strike the appropriate keys. Notice that the motion pattern right-left-right-left follows after each gong tone. It starts on a different pitch each time and therefore produces different intervals, yet the basic melodic contour remains the same—a rise in pitch followed by two descents. From this example it should be clear that contour alone is not enough information to create a melody: One must "anchor" the contour to particular pitches. (When this pattern starts from 3 in *pélog*, it involves skipping over the middle key on the *saron*, pitch 4, because that note does not "belong" in the pitch set appropriate to this *pathet*, or mode.)

Such examples also show that it is important to conceptualize melody in terms of contour rather than absolute pitches or interval sizes due to the two tuning systems and the variability within each system. Modern Javanese notation favors this approach because it gives no

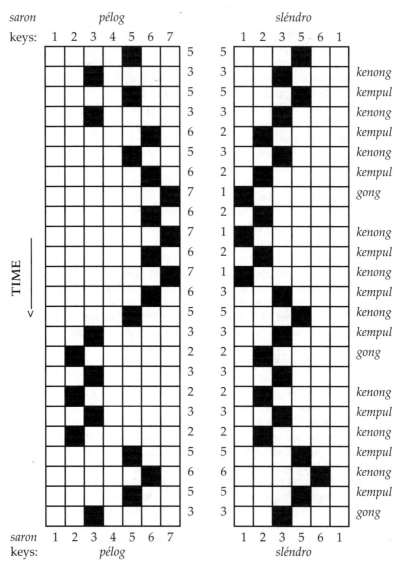

FIGURE 3.7A *Graph of the* balungan *(saron melody) for "Lancaran Singa Nebah" in* pélog *and* sléndro *in* irama lancar. *Each column represents a key on a* saron. *Reading from top to bottom, the black squares show the sequence in which the keys are struck. The two central columns of numbers also represent the melody.*

irama lancar:

$$\overset{+\qquad+\;(\;+\;)+\;(\;+\;)+\;(\;+\;)+}{.\,5\,.\,3\,.\,5\,.\,3\,.\,2\,.\,3\,.\,2\,.\,1\,.\,2\,.\,1\,.\,2\,.\,1\,.\,3\,.\,5\,.\,3\,.\,2\,.\,3\,.\,2\,.\,3\,.\,2\,.\,5\,.\,6\,.\,5\,.\,③}$$

irama 1:

$$\overset{+\qquad+\;(\;+\;)+\;(\;+\;)+\;(\;+\;)+}{\dot{1}653\dot{1}653232153215321353265326532565③}$$

irama 2: Each pair of notes is played twice. The colotomic pattern is stretched out.

For example: $\overset{+\;\;\;+\;\;(}{\dot{1}653}$ becomes $\dot{1}6\dot{1}65353$

FIGURE 3.7B *"Lancaran Singa Nebah Sléndro."*

approximations of *sléndro*   **approximations of *pélog***

2 3 2 1 2 3 2 1   2 3 2 1   2 3 2 1   2 3 2 1

FIGURE 3.8   *Some possible transnotations of 2321 in* sléndro *and* pélog.

specific information about absolute pitch or interval size. For instance, the melodic fragment 2321 can be played in both tuning systems, but its sound differs depending on the tuning system and on the gamelan. Transnotation onto a staff notation could yield any of the approximations shown in figure 3.8. Not one of these would be a completely accurate representation since Javanese tunings never correspond to the chromatic scale. Despite these acoustical variations, the sequence has the same musical meaning or identity. Its contour remains the same, rising a step before falling two steps.

American composer Lou Harrison, who wrote many pieces for gamelan, built his own instruments and tuned them to just intonation. In an article titled "Slippery Slendro," he wrote that he was disturbed by the variability of Javanese tuning because it meant that his pieces would sound different when played on different sets of instruments (Harrison, 1985). I have yet to meet a Javanese musician who is disturbed by this.

> **ACTIVITY 3.4**   *Listen to two versions of "Lancaran Singa Nebah" (CD tracks 19 and 26), played in* pélog *and* sléndro, *while following the notation in figure 3.7B (for* pélog*), the graphs in figure 3.7A, and the notation in figure 2.8 (for* sléndro*). Now stop the CD and try to sing the melody in each of these tunings. Listen again to check yourself. Do this repeatedly until you can hear and/or feel that the interval from pitch 3 to 5 in* pélog *is larger than in* sléndro *while the interval from 3 to 2 is smaller. This is not the only difference between* pélog *and* sléndro, *but it is a good place to start.*

Comparing the melodies in figure 3.7A, you probably noticed that they are not precisely the same. The most striking difference is that the *pélog* version uses 7 rather than 1. This causes some other differences in the melody that are useful for understanding certain tendencies in gamelan melodies. Since 7 is the highest pitch on the rightmost key of a *saron*,

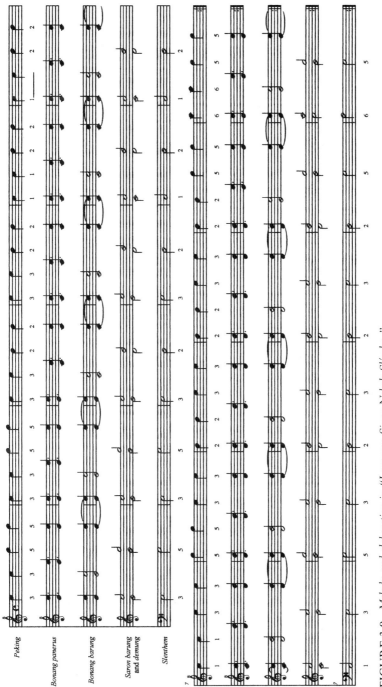

FIGURE 3.9 *Melody and elaboration in "Lancaran Singa Nebah Sléndro."*

there is no upper neighbor available. The lower neighbor is substituted to create the melody 6767 instead of 2121 in the *sléndro* version. Taking this a step further, the contour of the melody leading to gong 1 is inverted as 2321 becomes 6567. Look back at the graph in figure 3.7A to see that the *pélog* contour is a mirror image of the *sléndro* contour: The mallet moves left-right-right rather than right-left-left.

MELODY AND ELABORATION

Balungan, Peking, and Bonang. The word *balungan* is commonly used to refer to the type of melody I have been discussing, the one that is usually played on the medium and large *saron* as well as the *slenthem*. This is the part that is most often notated, if any part of a piece is committed to writing, and it is the only part that is played by several musicians together. Other musicians play either the sparser colotomic parts or the denser elaborating parts, so called because they tend to fill out the melodic line of the *balungan*. That *balungan* literally means "skeleton" indicates that it may not be the most important or fullest representation of the melody of a piece. Other parts are needed to put "flesh" on the melodic "bones." The *balungan* may be very prominent, particularly in condensed *irama* with a full gamelan; conversely, the *balungan* recedes greatly in prominence in an expansive *irama*. In a piece like "Lancaran Singa Nebah," which is played mainly at the more compressed levels of *irama*, the *balungan* remains prominent and there is relatively little scope for elaboration.

Even in such a simple piece as this *lancaran*, the *balungan* is not the only strand in the texture. In addition to the drumming and the colotomic parts that were described in the previous chapter, there are three additional strands played on the *peking* (small *saron*) and the two *bonang*.

> **ACTIVITY 3.5** *Study figure 3.9 to see typical ways in which the* bonang *and* peking *players create parts to play with the* balungan *in* sléndro. *Using this as a model, write out (in numbers) the* peking *and* bonang *parts for the following fragment of the* balungan *in* pélog: *53536567. Now listen to CD track 13 and try to hear these parts.*

Here, in the most elemental form, are two principles of elaboration: subdivision of the beat and repetition. The *peking* part elaborates the *balungan* in a very straightforward manner, simply playing each note twice. The *bonang* player, on the other hand, abstracts (or "flattens") the *balungan* by thinking ahead to the second note of each pair, playing that note twice, in octaves, off the beat (which is much simpler to do than to explain).

Note the timing of the *bonang* part. It changes to the next goal tone (*sèlèh*) before anyone else does; in this sense, it leads or anticipates. The musician seated at the *bonang panerus* plays those same notes (an octave higher, since the instrument is pitched an octave higher) and with a different rhythm, one that interlocks with the rhythm of the larger *bonang* and the *balungan* to enrich the rhythmic texture. So while the *bonang* parts abstract the pitch content of the *balungan*, they elaborate the rhythm.

What happens if the drummer slows the pace and switches from *irama* 1/2 to *irama* 1? The *balungan* players change their melody for this piece (but not necessarily for other pieces) by doubling their pace in relation to the beat and extending the elaboration of the basic *sèlèh*. In this manner 67 becomes 3567, 32 becomes 6532, etc. The fact that the *balungan* changes when the *irama* changes is not unusual, but this particular way of altering it is peculiar to this piece.

When the drummer cues the musicians to shift to a slower, more expansive *irama*, the *bonang* players do not continue to play a reduction of the *balungan* using octave technique; rather, they take pairs of notes and repeat each pair. This technique of elaboration is called *mipil* (literally, to do little by little). The phrase 3532 becomes 35353232 on the larger *bonang*. Note that this is a different type of doubling from that performed on the *peking*. On the smaller *bonang*, the player will base his or her part on a further doubling. In theory, the *saron* melody 35 generates 35353535 on the *bonang*, but in practice, players vary this repetitive figuration by omitting one or more notes. The upper half of figure 3.10 shows these parts for *irama* 1 while the lower shows the parts for *irama* 2, a set of time relationships that is twice as expansive as *irama* 1 (and four times as expansive as *irama lancar*; note that the *bonang* part may vary in some details).

In *irama* 1, the *peking* player continues to double the *balungan*, but if the *irama* expands again to *irama* 2, there is more scope for elaboration. The *balungan* 6532 generates the *peking* elaboration 6655665533223322, for instance.

ACTIVITY 3.6 *Write out the peking and bonang parts appropriate for the balungan 7653 played in irama 1. Now listen to CD track 19, starting at 0:29, and try to hear these parts. Can you formulate rules to explain the relationships between these three parts?*

Irama Tanggung (1)

```
bonang panerus  3 5 3 . 3 5 3 5 3 2 3 . 3 2 3 2
bonang          3   5 3   5 3   2 3   2
peking            3 3   5 5   3 3   2 2
balungan            3     5     3     2
```

Irama Dadi (2)

```
bonang panerus  3 5 3 . 3 5 3 . 3 5 3 . 3 5 3 5 3 2 3 . 3 2 3 . 3 2 3 . 3 2 3 2
bonang          3   5 3   5 3   . 3   5 3   2 3   . 3   2 3   3 2
peking            3 3   5 5   3 3   5 5   3 3   2 2   3 3   2 2
balungan            3     3           5     3           3     2
```

FIGURE 3.10 Peking, bonang, *and bonang panerus elaboration in irama 1 and 2.*

"Ladrang Asmaradana." "Lancaran Singa Nebah" has provided a starting point for learning about elaboration, but since it is not typical of the majority of Javanese gamelan pieces, I will continue the discussion of melody and melodic elaboration by moving on to "Ladrang Asmaradana," a longer, more complex piece. It is composed in *ladrang* form, based on a colotomic structure of 32 beats (see figure 2.3). All of the common colotomic instruments are sounded in this form, interlocking to form the *ladrang* pattern shown in figure 2.3.

Like any other *ladrang*, "Asmaradana" has a short melodic introduction that may be played solo on the *rebab*, as on CD track 26, or on *bonang* or *gendèr*. The drummer joins for the last eight beats of this introduction, regulating the tempo and cueing the other musicians to begin playing with the gong at the end of the introduction.

A performance of "Ladrang Asmaradana" usually begins in *irama* 1 and continues until the drummer slows to *irama* 2. This may happen in the first cycle or after one or more complete cycles. The drummer can expand the cycle further to *irama* 3 and even to *irama* 4. There are many options for this piece, which can be played in as many as four *irama* levels. The other musicians not only follow the drummer's cue to change tempo and *irama* but may alter the melodies they perform as well. This is most obvious for *bonang* playing technique and elaboration.

The two *bonang* players will use *mipil* elaboration while the drummer plays the large *kendhang gendhing,* but when they hear the *ciblon*, with its more complex playing style, they switch to an interlocking technique called *imbal*. Two *bonang* pitches alternate with two *bonang panerus* pitches to create a continuous rapid ripple of sound. For instance, while one plays pitches 1 and 3, the other plays 2 and 5 (or reverses the order to 5 and 2) in between, resulting in the melody 1235 or 1532. The musicians intersperse so-called flower patterns (*sekaran*) to lead to each *sèlèh* (see figure 3.11). These offer players the opportunity to select from a fairly extensive array of possibilities and even create new melodies. The main constraints on these flower patterns are duration and ending pitch. Interlocking parts are sometimes played on a pair of *saron*. You can hear this on CD track 26 beginning at 0:17 and moving twice as fast as the *balungan*.

On CD track 27, you can hear the drummer switch to the *ciblon* at 0:21 and the *bonang* players shift to *imbal* a few seconds later. They continue until the drummer goes back to the lower-pitched *kendhang gendhing* (with its small partner, the *ketipung*) at 1:17 when they immediately revert to *mipil* elaboration (of the sort shown in figure 3.10). Note that when the drummer started playing *ciblon*, he did not actually change

```
.2.5.2.5.2.5.2...2̊.2̊.2̊.2̊.2̊.2̊.2̊.

1 3 1 3 1 3 1 3 1̊ 1̊ 1̊ . 1̊ 1̊ 1̊ 1̊
imbal                    sekaran emphasizing 1
```

resulting melody:

```
1235123512351 23.1̊2̊1̊2̊1̊2̊.2̊1̊2̊1̊2̊1̊2̊1̊
```

```
.5.2.5.2.5.2.5.  3  5  6  1 .321516
                 .           .   .

1 3 1 3 1 3 1 3  3  5  6  1 .321516
imbal            .  .         sekaran emphasizing 6
```

resulting melody:

```
153215321532153  3̊  5̊  6̊  1̊ .3̊2̊1̊5̊1̊6̊
                 .   .         .    .
```

Key: ° = octave   1̊ = 1 and 1̇ played simultaneously

FIGURE 3.11 *Examples of* bonang imbal *(interlocking pattern) and* sekaran *("flower" patterns) that emphasize the* sèlèh *(goal tone). The* bonang panerus *part is shown above the* bonang barung *part and is written relative to its own range. Hence, the low 2 on the* bonang panerus *(with a dot beneath) corresponds to the middle register 2 on the* bonang barung *(with no dot).*

---

irama, but when he went back to the pair of drums a minute later, he drastically slowed the tempo down to *irama* 2.

The *saron peking* player is less affected by the drummer's shifts. The important consideration is the *irama,* not the liveliness of the drumming. In *irama* 1 the *peking* part doubles each note of the *saron* part. When *irama* 2 is reached, the *peking* player takes pairs of notes from the *saron* part and doubles them in the following manner: 21 becomes 22112211. If the *balungan* is stretched further, the *peking* player creates the same sort of patterning but interpolates neighboring pitches to fill in the spaces in the *balungan:* for . 2 . 1 The most likely *peking* part is 3322332233112211. You might think the *peking* player would play 3322332222112211, but the extensive repetition of 2 in the middle of this sequence breaks a tacit rule.

The *balungan* itself can change when the musicians shift to a more expansive *irama*. How does this work? Much as it did for "Lancaran Singa Nebah" but on a grander scale. As the drummer slows down from *irama* 2 to 3, a process begun eight beats before the gong, the length of each successive beat increases. By the time the gong is reached, the beat is about twice as long as it was at the beginning of the cycle. The *saron* players continue to play at this slower pace for the first *kenongan* (line ending with a *kenong* stroke; see figure 3.12 part B) and then double their pace, effectively returning to the speed they were playing before the drummer led them in the transition to *irama* 3. The colotomic players, however, continue to play at the slower, expanded pace, as you can see by the colotomic markings over the *balungan*.

Compare the *balungan* in part A of figure 3.12 with that in part B. Each of the four *kenongan* of B corresponds to the parallel *kenongan* in section A, but the type of correspondence differs. For instance, in the first *kenongan*, the sequence of notes is identical while the expansion involves replacing 5321 with 61326321 for the first half of the second *kenongan* but leaving the second half unchanged.

ACTIVITY 3.7 *Listen to CD track 27 as you follow the notation in figure 3.12. Write down the timing for each change of speed, and try to identify the* irama. *Write down which drums you hear in each* irama: *the medium-size* ciblon *or the pair of large and small drums. Listen for* mipil *and* imbal *played on* bonang, *noting which type of elaboration is played in each* irama. *Finally, note when you hear the male chorus and the female singers, singing solo or together. In chapter 4, you will learn more about what they are singing.*

"Ladrang Asmaradana" exemplifies each of the three themes of this book. The piece is immediately recognizable for any Javanese musician, yet there are infinite ways to perform it—the recording on CD track 27 is but one of them. Flexibility characterizes the confluence of piece, performance practice, and musicians. This is manifested, for instance, in the choice of *irama* and the number of repetitions of the gong cycle: The piece may be played in every *irama* except *irama lancar*, but musicians might use just one or two of them; the number of repetitions in a given *irama* is not fixed either. The singers may choose from a number of texts. Musicians playing instruments such as *rebab*, *gendèr*, and *gambang* have substantial flexibility in their choice of notes. All of these choices and

"Ladrang Asmaradana Sléndro Manyura"

buka: 3 2 2   .   3 2 2 3 1 3 2   .   1   .   ⑥

A) irama 1 or 2 (tanggung or dadi)

```
       -  +  -        -  +  -        ⌢
[:     2  1  2  6     2  1  2  3
                 ⌄              ⌢
       5  3  2  1     3  2  3  1
                 ⌄              ⌢
       6  3  2  1     3  2  1  6
                 ⌄
       5  3  2  1     3  2  1  ⑥  :]
```

irama 3 or 4 (wiled or rangkep) — two versions:

B) a partially expanded balungan

```
    -     +        -              -     +        -           ⌢
.   2  .  1    .   2  .  6    .   2  .  1    .   2  .  3
                         ⌄                                   ⌢
6   1  3  2    6   3  2  1    .   3  .  2    .   3  .  1
                         ⌄                                   ⌢
6   6  1  2    6   3  2  1    .   3  .  2    .   1  .  6
                         ⌄
5   3  5  3    6   3  2  1    .   3  .  2    .   1  .  ⑥
```

FIGURE 3.12 Balungan and Colotomic Parts for "Ladrang Asmaradana." The kethuk and kempyang parts are only shown for the first line of each section.

the possibilities they open up for the musicians are interconnected in numerous complex ways. You caught a glimpse of this when examining the connections between the expanded and condensed versions of the balungan.

If everything is so flexible, you may well wonder what is fixed and what distinguishes this piece as "Asmaradana." A sense of appropriateness guides the musicians in their choices. There are numerous performance conventions that dictate what can and cannot be done with this piece and whether "Asmaradana" is an appropriate choice for a given portion of a performance. The gong cycle with its colotomic parts is not open to substantial modification, so for a given *irama* the number of beats in the cycle is determined. The drum patterns appropriate for one *irama* cannot be played in another. Some patterns allow the drummer considerable scope for embellishment and variation, but their overall outline is fixed. The ratio between the faster moving parts and the beat is not open to individual choice—the *gambang* player, for instance, must play 8 notes to the beat in *irama* 2 and 16 in *irama* 3 while the *peking* player must play 4 and 8, respectively, in those two *irama*. The vocal parts and the playing techniques on instruments such as the *bonang* are also appropriate for one *irama* and not for others. The individual *saron* players do not spontaneously decide to play different versions of the melody simultaneously but strive to play the same version. Finally, the differences between these versions are not significant enough to stray from the basic melodic outline of "Asmaradana."

The *balungan* often serves as a reference point, a core of the piece, but its prominence in the overall sound of the ensemble changes in accordance with *irama* and drumming style. In any case, it is not thought of as *the* melody of the piece; rather, there are many simultaneously sounding melodies that are interdependent manifestations of the melodic essence or potential of the piece (see chapter 5). Among these strands, some of the vocal melodies associated with this piece play a central role in how musicians conceptualize the piece and how listeners perceive it. These melodies are the subject of the next chapter.

CHAPTER 4

Songs, Singers, and Gamelan

Listen to almost any commercial recording of gamelan made in Java and you will notice that the female singers' voices are prominent. Inspect the cover of the cassette or CD and you will find that the only performers named there, besides the group leader, are likely to be the female singers. Their photos may grace the cover, too. At several points in the recording, a male chorus is likely to be heard alongside the female soloist, and one or two pieces might even feature a solo male voice, but women's voices can be heard far more frequently. In live performances, too, the singers may be amplified while the instruments are not. Obviously this was not always the case. The advent of electricity changed many things in Java as elsewhere in the world.

Over the course of the twentieth century, the growing prominence of the singers due to amplification went hand in hand with an increase in the number of vocal-centered compositions that had begun in the late nineteenth century. The influence of popular song styles imported to or created in Indonesia has certainly played a part in this development. Yet despite these factors favoring vocal prominence, in many of the gamelan pieces performed to this day, the vocal parts are not considered to be any more important than the various instrumental strands with which they entwine.

SOCIAL ASPECTS OF SINGING

The traditional term for women who sing with gamelan is *pesindhèn*; their singing is called *sindhènan*. While many (including some of the singers themselves) still use the term, other words have been introduced because *pesindhèn* acquired negative connotations of licentiousness—singers stay out all night, traveling with a group of male musicians. Essentially euphemisms, these alternate appellations include *waranggana*, a literary term meaning "heavenly nymph," and *swarawati*, meaning "voice of feminine beauty." This renaming was part of a broader move in the middle of the twentieth century. As the new Republic of Indonesia established performing arts conservatories and then university-level academies, the new teaching staff sought to gain legitimacy and elevate the social status of gamelan music by renaming not only the *pesindhèn* but instrumentalists and male singers as well. Instead of *niyaga*, an instrumentalist was to be called *pangrawit*, maker of beautiful things, and male singers were dubbed *wiraswara* (heroic voice) rather than *penggérong*. Of these new names, only *pangrawit* had already existed in the language as a component in the names of certain court musicians such as my teacher Martopangrawit (see Sumarsam 1995: 124).

The questionable reputation of female singers was linked to the itinerant female performers who traveled around Java during Dutch colonial times, with a small gamelan that played for whoever would pay. Male "customers" would take turns dancing with the woman who also sang. Similar practices have been widespread in other parts of Java and in Bali. In *tayuban*, a popular form of entertainment at parties, male guests take turns dancing with professional female dancers. One of my oldest teachers, R. Ng. Mloyowidodo, told me how he and other relatively low-status men would wait many hours for their turn. He claimed that his wife would look on with pride from the women's quarters.

Dual competence in dancing and singing was also developed in other, more respectable venues. At the Mangkunagaran palace, a dance drama called Langen Driya, invented in the second half of the nineteenth century, required a cast of women who could dance and sing. There was no question of dancing with guests or patrons—this was a staged performance genre that told a story of medieval Java through dance, song, and gamelan accompaniment. "Ladrang Asmaradana" in something like its current form originated in this form of court entertainment.

Whatever the controversy over female gamelan singers' status and reputation, there can be no doubt that they are the best-known and best-paid performers other than shadow play puppeteers. Their fee for a performance may exceed the male instrumentalists' pay by a factor of 20 or more. They often sit in a place of prominence, and they have opportunities to sing featured solos while other musicians remain almost faceless members of the group. Yet there is also no question that they are objectified for the male gaze, on display in flamboyant colors, lavish clothes, makeup, and jewelry. In shadow play performances in particular, they are often expected to project a flirtatious image and are expected to keep their cool when they are subjected to comments (some stylized, some spontaneous) from male musicians and the *dhalang* during their solos. Male musicians with whom I have spoken over the years clearly have a highly developed appreciation for the singing of particular *pesindhèn*. At the same time, most of them consider themselves more knowledgeable than the singers about vocal art. These women truly occupy a conflicted position. Dissertations by Susan Walton and Nancy Cooper address these issues as well as female singers' struggles to gain and maintain control over their images and careers.

Men sing primarily as a chorus, the *gérong*. This male choral singing is so ubiquitous in gamelan performances today and so characteristic of the sound of the ensemble that I was surprised to learn that it is a far more recent practice than female *sindhènan*, probably developing only at the end of the nineteenth century (see Sumarsam 1995: 97ff for further discussion of this history). Within a gamelan performance, there are a few opportunities for male solos, but these soloists do not receive the same sort or amount of attention as the female singers.

There is little specialization among singers. They are generally expected to sing anything in the standard gamelan repertoire, and there is a steady flow of new pieces that singers learn primarily from notation or recordings. Unlike Western-derived choruses, which divide female voices into sopranos and altos and male voices into tenors and basses, all singers are expected to cover the same range, which is a bit more than two octaves. For most gamelan tunings, a relatively high voice (roughly equivalent to a soprano or tenor) is more appropriate than a low one.

All singers use some ornamentation, ranging from vibrato to quick turns and dips. *Pesindhèn* may become known for their particular vocal qualities in addition to their abilities. Timbre is not standardized. Some singers have relatively piercing voices, while others are relatively mellow. Singing in a nasal head voice is common, but not all singers do so. No matter how much the vocal timbre varies, it always differs markedly from the soft, smooth, and relatively low-pitched crooning featured in most Indonesian pop songs.

POETRY, SONG, AND GAMELAN

To understand Javanese song, it is necessary to consider connections with other forms of cultural expression such as literature, philosophy, theater, and dance. The principle of interconnectedness is nowhere more apparent than in the association of singing and poetry.

Until recently Javanese *tembang*—the word means both poem and song—was written to be sung for a listening audience rather than read silently by an individual. Much of it was written in poetic meters called *macapat* (pronounced maw-chaw-pat). Each of these meters is associated with specific melodies. Since the length of a stanza (and its constituent lines) is defined by the meter, any melody that fits one verse in a given meter will fit all others in that meter. Thus, knowing these melodies, one can sing any poem written in *macapat* meters. Social gatherings at which people take turns singing consecutive verses of a long poem have become less common than they were a few generations ago (documented in Arps 1992), but knowledge of the meters and their melodies is widespread among musicians and is applied to a large body of poetry written from the late eighteenth century to the present. In this chapter I shall focus on song in the context of gamelan performance.

A *macapat* meter is defined by the number of lines in a stanza, the number of syllables in each line, and the ending vowel of each line (any consonant following that vowel does not affect the meter). For instance, any verse in Pangkur meter will have the same number of lines per stanza, the same distribution of syllables, and the same pattern of final vowels as the first verse in figure 4.1, the famous opening of the *Serat Wédhatama*, a nineteenth-century didactic poem attributed to Prince Mangkunagara IV, who ruled from 1857 to 1881. Note how, in addition to following the rules of the poetic meter, the author used alliteration extensively, binding the words in a twisting chain of closely linked sounds. In the first verse, the author promises to unfold the secret knowledge of the kings of Java through song. In the second excerpt from this poem, he says that this secret knowledge must be achieved through practice and the suppression of evil passions (CD track 28).

The *macapat* meters are usually associated with a particular range of affects or types of poetic content. For instance, Pangkur is appropriate for passages about infatuated love. Asmaradana is also used when the subject is love, but it is more appropriate when the situation is grave, as it is in the passage quoted in figure 4.1: in this verse Damarwulan, a medieval hero, bids adieu to his distant love as he faces almost certain death.

A lengthy poem is likely to have several sections, each being in a different *macapat* meter and therefore requiring a change of melody. The *Serat Wédhatama*, for instance, uses four meters, with numerous stanzas in each. Though it is rarely sung in its entirety, select verses from this widely known classic of Javanese literature are sung in most gamelan performances; in addition to *macapat*, some poems in longer meters—and often in more archaic language—are sung, usually as a solo introduction to a gamelan composition.

Unlike songs in many other musical practices around the world, relatively few Javanese gamelan pieces have specific texts. For most

Macapat Pangkur

Line Number	Number of Syllables	Final Vowel	Sample verse from *Serat Wédhatama*
1	8	a	Mingkar mingkur ing angkara
2	11	i	Akarana karenan mardi siwi
3	8	u	Sinawung resmining kidung
4	7	a	Sinuba sinukarta
5	12	u	Mrih kretarta pakartining ngèlmu luhung
6	8	a	Kang tumrap nèng tanah jawa
7	8	i	Agama ageming aji

Macapat Pucung

Line Number	Number of Syllables	Final Vowel	Sample Verse from *Serat Wédhatama*
1	4	u	Ngèlmu iku
2	8	u	Kalakoné kanthi laku
3	6	a	Lekasé lawan kas
4	8	i	Tegesé kas nyantosani
5	12	a	Setya budya pangekesé dur angkara

Macapat Asmaradana

Line Number	Number of Syllables	Final Vowel	Sample Verse from *Langen Driya*
1	8	i	Anjasmara ari mami
2	8	a	Mas mirah, kulaka warta
3	8	o	Dasihmu tan wurung layon
4	8	a	Anèng kutha Prabalingga
5	8	a	Prang tandhing lan Urubisma
6	8	u	Karia mukti, wong ayu
7	8	a	Pun kakang pamit palastra

FIGURE 4.1 *Examples of* macapat *meters. The second example is sung by Midiyanto on CD track 28.*

pieces, the singers can choose from a large body of texts in the appropriate *macapat* meter. The poetic structure is almost always preserved in performance. This means that a line of poetry corresponds to a sung phrase (or pair of phrases). Furthermore, these phrases are generally shaped to correspond with the colotomic structure of the accompanying *gendhing*.

This correspondence is clear in "Ketawang Subakastawa," a widely performed traditional piece of unknown age and provenance. This piece is based on the 16-beat *ketawang* cycle, which consists of two 8-beat phrases (*kenongan*), unlike the four phrases in a *ladrang* and most other forms (see figure 2.3). Like most other pieces in *ketawang* form, "Subakastawa" begins with a cycle (labeled *umpak* in figure 4.2) that is played once or twice in the low register before the male chorus, the *gérong*, begins to sing in the *ngelik* section. As the musicians repeat the *umpak*, you should be able to hear the *rebab* soar up to the high register at 0:53 to cue the other musicians to proceed to the *ngelik* section. *Ngelik* refers to the high register.

ACTIVITY 4.1 *Listen to the recording of "Ketawang Subakastawa" that you heard in chapter 2 (CD track 10). This is an unusually short performance that goes through the piece just once. Study the notation with the recording. Ignoring the female singer for the moment, follow figure 4.2 as the* gérong *sing their part. Now sing along with the recording. Feel the phrasing: two phrases in each line of notation, the first ending on* kenong *(middle of the line) and the second on* gong *(end of the line).*

The text "midering rat," taken from another work by Prince Mangkunagara IV (*Serat Manuhara*), is just one of several popular poems in the *macapat* meter Kinanthi that are known by all singers and sung in almost any gamelan performance. Kinanthi is a particular favorite for composing *gérongan* melodies because its structure is more symmetrical than other *macapat*, consisting of six lines of equal length, eight syllables apiece. This means that it is easier to fit to the regular phrase lengths of a *ketawang* or *ladrang* than an irregular meter like Pangkur (see figure 4.1), whose poetic lines differ greatly in length and total an odd number.

Aside from the choice of text, the members of the male chorus do not have much flexibility. Since they must sing their part in unison,

"Ketawang Subakastawa Sléndro Sanga"
buka played on gendèr
umpak (played twice on CD track 10)

ngelik

Midering rat ange- la-ngut

La-la- na nja- jah ne- ga-ri

Mubeng tepi- ning sa-mo-dra

Su-mengka ang- graning wu-kir

A-na-la-sak wa-na- wa- sa

Tumurun mring jurang tre- bis

Midering rat angelangut
Lalana njajah negari
Mubeng tepining samodra
Sumengka anggraning wukir
Analasak wanawasa
Tumurun mring jurang trebis

Traveling around the world to far off places
Wandering to many places
Going around the edge of the ocean
Climbing to the peak of a mountain
Traversing the thick forest
Descending into a deep ravine.

individual elaboration is not valued. The female singer, on the other hand, has far more freedom. When the *gérong* sings, she is supposed to sing the same text, but she lags behind, her timing flexible, and sings around—rather than on—the beat. She shapes a melody that follows the general contour of the choral melody without being an exact copy.

What about the first part of the piece, the *umpak*, where the *gérong* is silent? Here the *pesindhèn* has still greater freedom, selecting short texts from a stock of *wangsalan* and also picking melodic phrases appropriate to the musical context. A *wangsalan* is a riddle consisting of a pair of 12-syllable lines. You can hear an example in the first two *gongan* of "Ketawang Subakastawa" (CD track 10). The *pesindhèn* Sri Sularni sings "Trahing nata garwa risang dananjaya / dèn prayitna sabarang aywa sembrana," which Midiyanto helped me translate as "The blood of kings, the wife of Arjuna / be cautious all of you, don't be careless." The two epithets in the first line of the riddle refer to Sembadra, who is the daughter of King Basudewa and wife of Prince Arjuna. The answer to the riddle comes at the end of the second line. The word *sembrana* (careless or rude) sounds like the name Sembadra.

The performance of this *wangsalan* in the unfolding structure of "Ketawang Subakastawa" demonstrates both flexibility and appropriateness. Sri Sularni did not have to reproduce a specific rhythm or melodic contour but she had to fit her singing to the structure of the piece, aiming for the goal tones (*sèlèh*) at the main structural points where *kenong* and gong sound. She also needed to sing a melody appropriate to *pathet sléndro sanga*, the mode (*pathet*) of the piece. She waited for the drummer to slow to *irama* 2 before she began to sing. Since she needed to fit the first line of the *wangsalan* into the first *gongan* she sang it straight through, ending just after the gong. In the next *gongan* the tempo had settled, so she had time to divide the second line of the *wangsalan* into two parts tied to the two most important points in the cycle: a 4-syllable segment ending on *kenong* and an 8-syllable segment ending on gong. Between these points she interspersed short phrases that are not part of the *wangsalan*, singing *ya mas, ya mas* (yes brother) at 0:36 and *éman, éman, éman* (what a pity) at 0:52. Such "filler" is sung very frequently in conjunction with *wangsalan*.

Wangsalan have been orally transmitted for generations, but it is also increasingly common to write them down. Almost all female singers

FIGURE 4.2 *(opposite) The* gérong *part for "Ketawang Subakastawa" with* bal-ungan *and colotomic gongs. The text, one of several that can be sung to this melody, is taken from* Serat Manuhara *by Mangkunagara IV. The* kethuk *and* kempyang *parts are notated only in the first line, but follow the same pattern for every line thereafter.*

keep notebooks filled with lyrics, including both *wangsalan* and specific song texts such as "midering rat" and other *macapat* texts. This enables considerable flexibility in performance because words are not tied to melodies. It is not uncommon to see a *pesindhèn* singing while leafing through her notebook for the next set of lyrics.

Numerous other pieces are composed in *ketawang* form. Most follow the model heard here, performed in a sedate *irama* 2, with alternation between *umpak* and *ngelik* sections. Since many *ketawang* share the same *umpak* section, you may not know which *ketawang* is being played until the musicians reach the *ngelik* section. Every *ketawang* has a unique *ngelik* with a unique *gérongann* melody. Some, such as "Ketawang Puspawarna" (Wade 2004 and track 8 on the CD accompanying that book), also have specially composed texts.

The prolific and very popular musician Ki Nartosabdho (1925–1985), who greatly influenced Javanese performing arts from the 1950s to the present day, took the traditional composition, "Ketawang Subakastawa," and created a new arrangement. He transposed it from *sléndro* to *pélog* (a common transformation for other pieces) and added vocal parts with new lyrics in colloquial rather than poetic Javanese, eschewing *macapat* meters. The text does not speak in mystical terms, as older poems often did, but offers a naturalistic description of the beauty of birds, mountains, forests, and crops in the fields. Nartosabdho also added contrast by switching to lively *ciblon* drumming for the *umpak* section when it recurs.

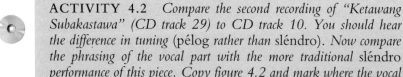

ACTIVITY 4.2 *Compare the second recording of "Ketawang Subakastawa" (CD track 29) to CD track 10. You should hear the difference in tuning (pélog rather than sléndro). Now compare the phrasing of the vocal part with the more traditional sléndro performance of this piece. Copy figure 4.2 and mark where the vocal phrases on CD track 29 begin and end. Write a brief description of the differences. How do the vocal phrases fit the colotomic structure? How independent is the* pesindhèn *in Nartosabdho's version?*

Both female and male singers have other parts to play in a gamelan performance. During passages with *ciblon* drumming that have no composed vocal part, the male singers will clap interlocking patterns to fill in the beat and enhance the liveliness of the drumming. In some pieces, it is appropriate for the male singers to add stylized calls. Some are like carefully controlled cries or shouts, purportedly derived from hunting calls (Brown and Toth 1971); others are actual melodies with a few words. The cries or shouts herald the sounding of the main colotomic instruments — gong, *kenong,* and *kempul.*

ACTIVITY 4.3 *Listen again to the beginning of the* talu, *the overture to a shadow play (CD track 21). The first piece in this medley is "Ladrang Sri Katon." At 0:43 you should hear the men call out just after the* kempul *stroke and before the gong. They then sing their regular vocal part (which I will discuss presently). At 1:48 they sing a short phrase leading to the* kempul *stroke. When do you hear another one of these calls or short phrases? It ends at 3:26.*

"Ladrang Sri Katon" offers another opportunity to hear standard practice for male and female singers. Composed in a 32-beat *ladrang* form, it spans two gong cycles. The main choral part is sung in the second *gongan,* using a text that is probably the most commonly sung text of all, used in hundreds of pieces in *ladrang* form. It consists of a series of riddles and puns similar to the *wangsalan* sung by *pesindhèn,* but cast in a different form: four lines of eight syllables apiece. Notice that in this piece the first and second lines of the choral melody share the same ending while the third and fourth lines are identical throughout. This is an unusually repetitive vocal part.

ACTIVITY 4.4 *Copy the* balungan *notated in figure 4.3, and mark in the phrases of the* pesindhèn *while listening to CD track 21. Note once again how the* pesindhèn *sings the same text as the* gérong *but lags behind and improvises a somewhat different melody. In the other* gongan, *she sings* wangsalan, *as she did in the first* gongan *of "Ketawang Subakastawa" (CD track 10). Try to show when she stops and starts relative to the* balungan *and the male singers. Now compare that to the* ngelik *section on the 1930s recording of "Ladrang Sri Katon" in* pélog *(CD track 5 contains only the* ngelik*). The choral melody is changed to accommodate the change from* sléndro *to* pélog; *the* balungan *has been modified slightly, too. How does the relationship between female and male vocal lines differ?*

The next piece in the *talu* overture medley is in *ketawang* form, like "Ketawang Subakastawa." It therefore has a 16-beat cycle divided into two 8-beat *kenongan,* but unlike "Subakastawa," its *balungan* is fuller, with

"Ladrang Sri Katon Sléndro Manyura"

first gongan   *buka*

```
             3 2 2   .   3 2 2 3 1 2 2 1   6̣

 .   2̣   +   .   |   -   2 2 3 2 2 1   +̣ 2   ⌒6

 .   2̣       .       .       2       1   ⌒6

 .   2̣       .       .       2       1   ⌒6

 .   3̣       .       .       3       6   ⌒2
```

ngelik

```
 .   5̣   .       .       5       6   3

 .   5̣   .   2̣   6   5   3   3 6  1̇6̇5̇  3
      Pa - ra -  bé   Sang   Sma – ra   ba -  ngun
```

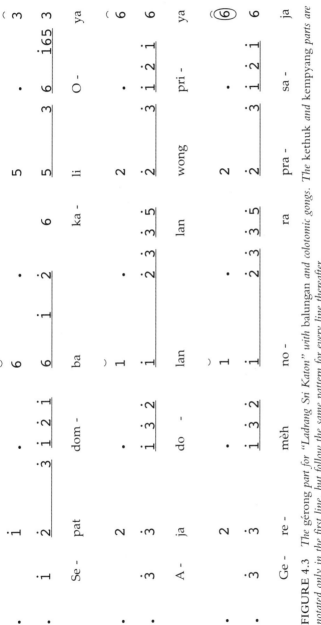

FIGURE 4.3 *The gérong part for "Ladrang Sri Katon" with balungan and colotomic gongs. The kethuk and kempyang parts are notated only in the first line, but follow the same pattern for every line thereafter.*

rebab	653	3	56	i̇				i̇2	26	6i̇23	i̇	i̇2	2̇	23321	6i̇	i̇26	i̇	i̇	i̇	i̇
pesindhèn	6	5	3	•	•	•	•	2̇3	2̇	i̇	2̇	.6536	•	2̇3	2̇i̇	2̇	66	5356	i̇
								Punapa ta			mirah ingsun			prihatin was—pa gung				mijil		
gérong	•	•	3	3	35	6	.i̇2	.3i̇2̇i̇	6	•	•	3̇3	3̇2̇i̇	•	i̇i̇.66	i̇2̇2̇	i̇			
			Pu-na-pa ta —			mirah	ing-sun			Priha-tin was —		pa gung mi —jil								
slenthem & gongs	⑥	3	3	•	5	6	3	5	6	•	•	5	6	i̇	3	2	1	⑥	i̇	i̇

FIGURE 4.4 *Excerpt from "Ketawang Suksma Ilang" performed by Sudarsi (pesindhèn) and Midiyanto (rebab) with other members of Hardo Budoyo (CD track 21, 4:13–4:51). This is the beginning of a frequently sung text in kinanthi meter in which the exiled prince Rama asks his love Sita why she is crying.*

a note on every beat. It is also treated differently in this case, with a cue from the drummer telling most of the musicians to stop playing and let the singers, *rebab*, and *gendèr* sound clearly in a softer, more transparent texture. This offers a perfect opportunity to hear the intertwining of *rebab*, *gérong*, and *pesindhèn*, each performing a different version of the melody, unique in its timing and details of pitch but conforming to the same *sèlèh* (goal tones) and general melodic contours (see figure 4.4, which corresponds to the segment from 4:13 to 4:51 on CD track 21). The text is another widely sung example of the Kinanthi *macapat* meter, six lines of eight syllables.

ACTIVITY 4.5 *Now listen to the rest of the* Talu, *after the* ketawang *(which ends at 5:47). Hear how the* pesindhèn *recedes into the background, singing only* wangsalan *and "filler" as the* saron, bonang, *and colotomic gongs come into the sonic foreground. When they reach their greatest intensity, the singing stops altogether. What is the time code?*

CONCLUSION

Javanese singing with gamelan exemplifies the three themes of flexibility, appropriateness, and interconnectedness. Female singers have considerable flexibility, not to improvise freely but to choose texts and melodic phrases from as large a stock as they have amassed. This should be done with a sense of appropriateness to the performance context, the piece, and the style in which it is being performed. Other musicians can be quite critical of singers whose choices they find inappropriate. The male singers who perform as *gérong* have far less flexibility because they must make their voices match and sing the same text and melody, preferably with all the same nuances. This applies, too, in the many instances that *pesindhèn* sing as a group, with or without the men. Song texts taken from famous literary works and used in various musical genres strengthen the sense of interconnectedness of the arts. Intertextuality is pervasive.

The types of singing described in this chapter are central to Javanese musical practice, but they do not by any means represent its entirety. In chapter 6, for instance, I will discuss the contrasting types of vocals sung by the *dhalang* in theatrical performances, but first I turn to the elaborating parts that so often entwine with the vocals.

CHAPTER 5

Melodic Elaboration and Training in the Arts

Many threads interweave to form the rich texture of a full gamelan performance. Gongs sounding in different timbres and registers "cradle" the rhythm by delineating a colotomic structure, the drums guide the rhythm, the melody is underpinned by the *balungan* that is usually played on *saron* and *slenthem*, and relatively simple elaborations on this melody are played on a pair of *bonang* and the *saron peking*. Much of the time, a female singer adds her voice to the mix, and a choral part may be sung in certain sections. In addition to all of these, there may be half a dozen more strands, each played by an individual musician on a different type of instrument. It is the melodies played on these instruments that I will discuss in this chapter, focusing on the two most important ones—the *rebab* and the *gendèr* (see figure 3.1). At the end of the chapter, I discuss the diverse and changing institutions and methods involved in the formation and transmission of the musical knowledge needed to play these parts.

REBAB, GENDÈR, AND OTHER ELABORATING INSTRUMENTS

You already encountered the melodic entwining of *rebab* and voices (see figure 4.4). While *rebab, pesindhèn,* and *gérong* followed the same basic path, ascending and descending to the same goal tones, each did so in a somewhat different way, particularly regarding rhythm and the nuances of the melody—a clear case of heterophony. The male chorus sang in strict coordination with the pulse, coinciding frequently with the *balungan*; the *pesindhèn* lagged behind while the *rebab* (played here by Midiyanto) shifted in relation to the other parts, sometimes anticipating, other times coinciding or even lagging. This is typical for the *rebab* part, which is thought to represent best the essence of the piece. When Pak Cokro first taught me to play *rebab*, he talked about choices:

to lead the *balungan*, to lead the singers, or to play one's own line. Others also recognize the *rebab*'s leadership: It is termed the "leader of the melody" (*pamurba lagu*) in Martopangrawit's classification of gamelan instruments (1984). In traditional Solonese gamelan repertoire, the majority of pieces are classified as *gendhing rebab*, introduced and led by the *rebab* (in conjunction with the drummer, of course). The instrument is considered particularly difficult because of the playing technique and the deep knowledge of the repertoire that the *rebab* player ought to have.

The *rebab* is strung with a single wire that is stretched from a tuning peg down the length of the instrument, wrapped around the foot, and then brought up the neck again to the other tuning peg. The resulting two "strings" pass over a thin bridge, carved of wood, which rests on the face of the resonator. This resonator, carved out of wood (but formerly made of coconut shell), is faced with a thin skin made of cow or goat bladder. Balancing the instrument on a rounded "foot," the player fingers these two strings lightly "in the air" rather than pressing them to the neck. The right hand tenses the loosely strung bow, taking considerable control over nuances of volume and tone.

The *rebab* has a relatively large range, spanning more than two octaves (see figure 3.6). This is precisely the range necessary to encompass the melodies of Javanese gamelan compositions. It is divided into three overlapping registers: low, medium, high. Indicating the appropriate register to the singers and instrumentalists is one of the most important ways that the *rebab* player exercises leadership. Because the *saron* and *slenthem* are limited to a one-octave range (give or take a note or two), the *balungan* as played on these instruments is "compressed." The melody 2165, which might be played as a stepwise descent on the *rebab* (moving either from 2 down to low 5 or from high 2 down to 5 in the middle register), is "folded" into the *saron* range, moving from 2 down to 1, skipping up to 6, and then moving down to 5. In such passages, it is crucial that the *rebab* player know and show which melody is implied: high or low.

ACTIVITY 5.1 *Listen again to "Ketawang Subakastawa" (CD track 10), focusing your attention on the* rebab. *The rebab melody is mainly in the low register to begin with. When does it move to the high register? Now listen again, trying to follow both the* rebab *and* pesindhèn. *Does she imitate the rebab player's first shift to the high register?*

When the *rebab* player moved to the high register at the end of the second *gongan* on CD track 10, he was giving a cue to continue to the *ngelik* section rather than play the *umpak* again. In pieces such as "Subakastawa," the *ngelik* always begins in the high register and features a choral part; its onset is always cued by the *rebab*.

From a musician's perspective, the parts played on *rebab* and *gendèr* are the heart of *gendhing*. While the *rebab* player leads the melody by indicating its register and pointing ahead to important goal tones, the *gendèr* player complements that with patterns that support the *rebab* line or enrich it with countermelodies. Together, they interpret the modal implications of the piece and indicate their conception(s) of the *lagu*, the "inner melody" of the piece. Neither is limited to following the *balungan*, though fairly regular convergence with it is expected.

> ACTIVITY 5.2 *Listen again to the soft section in the middle of CD track 21 (3:41 to 5:48) and try to pick out the* gendèr *in this relatively sparse texture. Can you hear how it weaves around the melody of the* rebab?

The playing idioms of *rebab* and *gendèr* differ greatly. The sustained *rebab* melody generally moves at a slower pace than the *gendèr* line but follows every nuance of the melodic flow of the piece. Its rhythm tends to be far less regular. The *gendèr* part is mainly polyphonic, a melody played by the left hand set against a subsidiary part played by the right hand. When playing *gendèr*, musicians tend to think in terms of moving gracefully from one goal tone to the next rather than responding to every twist and turn in the melodic flow of the piece as the *rebab* player does. They do so by means of patterns, called *céngkok*, discussed below.

The other elaborating parts, played on *suling, gambang, siter,* and *gendèr panerus*, are related in various ways to the *rebab* and *gendèr* melodies while exemplifying individual instrumental idioms. Melodies played on the *suling*, an end-blown flute, are relatively free rhythmically, like those of the *rebab*, but more sporadic due to the pauses that are idiomatic (stylistically appropriate) to the instrument. The *suling* adds a beautiful floating quality to the ensemble but is considered far less essential than *rebab* or *gendèr*. Easily made and easily cracked or lost, *suling* cannot be retuned to fit different ensembles, so it is not uncommon to find a gamelan played without *suling* (or with an out-of-tune *suling*). For instance, when I made recordings for this book with Midiyanto's group in Eromoko, no *suling* was available.

The other instrumental idioms, most of which can be heard individually on CD track 25, are radically different from the *rebab* and far more similar to the *gendèr*. They involve striking or plucking notes in time to the precise rhythmic grid guided by the drummer and demarcated by the colotomic parts. *Gambang, siter,* and *gendèr panerus* are all played rapidly, their characteristic density twice that of the *gendèr* idiom. The ratio to the main pulse depends, of course, on the *irama*.

ACTIVITY 5.3 *Listen again to CD track 25, the special recording of "Ladrang Asmaradana" that features each elaborating instrument in turn, using the* irama *3 section of the piece. The vocal solo substitutes for the first line of this section (see figure 3.12B). Listen to the various elaborating instruments in relation to both the* balungan *and the singer. You should be able to hear each one coincide with the* balungan *at least every four beats (seven seconds). The singer arrives at each of these goal tones several beats later.*

The *gambang* (see figure 3.5) has the largest range and is therefore most conducive to following the *rebab*'s lead in terms of register, but its patterns are otherwise more closely related to those of the *gendèr*. It is the only xylophone in the gamelan; its keys are made of hard wood and struck with two long, thin mallets made of water buffalo horn for flexibility and tipped with wooden disks padded with rope and cloth to give a warmer sound than hard mallets would produce.

ACTIVITY 5.4 *Compare* gendèr *and* gambang *idioms on CD track 30 while following figure 5.1. This track offers a good opportunity to review* irama, *too. The first part is in* irama *1, the second in* irama *2. Both* gendèr *and* gambang *parts double in density relative to the melody played on the* saron. *For the sake of simplicity, I have omitted some of the rhythmic nuances from these transcriptions.*

The *siter* (a plucked zither) (see figure 3.5) is often part of a gamelan but can also be played alone or in small ensembles, such as the trio of zithers you heard on CD track 7. Made in several sizes with several names (I will use *siter*, which sounds most like zither), the instrument is played with the thumbnails. Other fingers are used to damp strings after they are played or right as they are plucked. This is a versatile type of instrument whose idiom is far from fixed. It can be played in irama 1 (tanggung)

saron	6	5	3	2	**1**	3	2	1	**6**

gendèr 5 6 5 3 6 . 56 i 5 6 5 i 5 6 i 6
        . 2612 . . .1261 65. 3 5 6 . 16216.

gambang 6561612636563212132165353565356.

irama 2 (dadi)

saron	6	5	3	2	**1**	3	2	1	**6**

gendèr 5 6 .5 . 5 i 5 3 6 i 6 . .56 i .6.56 i 2 .i2 6 5 . 5 i 5 6 i 6
        . . 1 .16 126 5 3 . .56 2 161 161 . 2 6 3 . 3 532 .16 5 3 . 56356.

gambang 66211212321212123656162i6336563216121612353656261221321653535356356

FIGURE 5.1 The last kenongan of "Ladrang Asmaradana" played by Midiyanto (gendèr) and Heri Purwanto (gambang). The gendèr and gambang parts for each irama are played consecutively on CD track 30 but shown together here for the sake of comparison. Only the first iteration for each instrument in irama 2 is shown here. The goal tones (sèlèh) 1 and 6 are shown in boldface.

a highly repetitive manner or with considerable variety and finesse. Rather than playing long melodies that lead to goal tones, a *siter* player often repeats a short rippling pattern, like the *imbal* played on *bonang*, followed by a short melody ending on the goal tone. This manner of playing enables a musician to play pieces with which he is not altogether familiar, creating a steady sound while listening to the other musicians for clues to the course of the melody. It also means that the instrument is easier to learn than the *gendèr, gambang,* or *rebab*, enabling Pak Cokro to begin playing when he was five. The *gendèr panerus*, a smaller version of the *gendèr* that is tuned one octave higher, is played in a very similar manner. Rather than playing an independent part in each hand, much of the time a musician will use two thumbs (on the *siter*) or two mallets (on the *gendèr panerus*) to create a single melody.

CÉNGKOK, VARIATION, AND THE TRANSMISSION OF MUSICAL KNOWLEDGE

The idiom for each of the elaborating parts consists of playing techniques appropriate to each instrument and of a stock of basic patterns, called *céngkok*, which can be performed in specific situations. The playing techniques vary only a little from one performer to the next. For the *gendèr*, for instance, the techniques include ways of striking the keys with the padded mallets and damping them with the fingers and sides of the hand. *Rebab* techniques include bowing and fingering choices.

The stock of patterns associated with a particular instrument is also broadly shared among musicians, though it usually differs enough for knowledgeable performers to distinguish one musician's playing from another. Individual musicians may develop particular ways of playing a given pattern that are unique, but rarely does a musician play something that is not recognizably related to commonly performed patterns.

How do *céngkok* fit a given musical context? The three themes of flexibility, appropriateness, and interconnectedness offer means to understand the basic workings of these patterns. Each pattern is flexible: It can be manifested in many ways, with variations large and small, while remaining recognizably "the same." It can be expanded or contracted depending on the *irama*. Many patterns can be transposed and otherwise transformed to fit different musical contexts. Such transformations conform to ideas of appropriateness in a given context—an issue where musicians may disagree. Whatever their differences of opinion, they would probably agree on the principle that each pattern is appropriate for performance in certain musical contexts, defined by *pathet* (mode), *sèlèh* (goal tone), *lagu* (melody), *irama*, register, and overall affect or feeling (*rasa*). This last consideration, *rasa*, is intimately linked to the drumming—just as the *bonang* players switch between *mipil* and *imbal* playing styles depending on whether the drummer plays the big *kendhang gendhing* or the livelier *ciblon*, so do the other musicians perform relatively sedate or lively versions of patterns. It also has to do with the consensus about particular pieces; for example some are considered to be livelier, others more serious.

The interconnectedness that pervades Javanese gamelan manifests in the many correspondences among the various playing idioms and their stocks of patterns. Many *céngkok* for the *gendèr* are linked to patterns played on other instruments and to certain vocal phrases with which they may coincide. It is this last correspondence, in fact, that musicians use to give names to some *gendèr* patterns, calling them by the words of related vocal phrases. The connections among the various idioms create a lot of simultaneous variety within a fairly unified texture. They enable musicians to apply their knowledge of a piece to any of the instruments that they have mastered. In other words, if a musician knows how to play *gendèr* for a particular piece, for instance, and also knows the basic *gambang* idiom, he or she will be able to play that piece on *gambang* based on correspondences between the *gendèr* and *gambang* idioms. This is quite different from the challenge facing a violinist in a string quartet who wants to play the viola part. Such similarities are apparent even in the brief examples transcribed in figure 5.1. Note that Midiyanto and Heri approach the *sèlèh* 6 in *irama* 2 with the same melody: 56356. They did not plan this—it is simply evidence of the overlap between the two idioms and the connections between parallel *céngkok*.

Another crucial effect of the pervasive patterning of elaborating instrument idioms is that musicians can transfer their knowledge from one piece to another with relative ease. How does this work? Knowing how to play *gendèr* for "Ladrang Asmaradana," a musician can apply the same patterns to analogous passages in other pieces, making educated guesses as to which *céngkok* are appropriate. Such analogies are not always appropriate, of course. Midiyanto recounted an experience as a new student at the arts academy when Martopangrawit criticized him for playing in this manner because he did not know that the piece in question, "Gendhing Ela-ela Kalibeber," had special *gendèr* parts in certain passages.

Nonetheless, the possibility of playing one piece by analogy to others is so strong that the state schools for the arts took it as one of the bases

for their curriculum. Students learn a small core of pieces in their first
year and then apply the same patterns to other pieces in subsequent
years. Teachers at these schools have published catalogs of basic patterns for the *gendèr* and the *gambang* that sort the patterns by *pathet*
(mode) and *sèlèh* (ending pitch). Each *céngkok* must be conceived as a set
of closely related possibilities, for there is no one fixed form that stands
as the "correct" or standard version.

The *gendèr* (see figure 3.1) has the most extensively developed and
named set of *céngkok* and therefore serves as a reference point both in
practice and in theoretical discussions. Most of its basic *céngkok* are four
beats long, with a few being twice that length; however, all of these
patterns can be parsed into smaller units. The ability to combine these
patterns and manipulate their parts is fundamental to Javanese musicianship. This is true for players of the *gambang* and other elaborating
instruments. *Gambang* patterns will provide a simpler example here
since they are monophonic—except for slight variations, the player
plays the same melody in both hands, one octave apart.

ACTIVITY 5.5 *Compare the* gambang *parts that Heri Purwanto
played in irama 1 and 2 (see figure 5.1 and CD track 30) by copying
them out to line up similar passages. In* irama *2, successive goal tones
are twice as far apart in time as they are in* irama *1, so when a piece
expands from one* irama *to another,* gambang *players often find themselves filling in spaces between the* sèlèh*. What did Heri do? Note that
he used the same pattern to arrive at* sèlèh *1 in both* irama*. Did he play
the same pattern to* sèlèh *6, in both* irama*, too? Circle the* balungan
notes with which he coincided. Are they the same in the two irama*?*

*If you would like a further challenge, try to answer the same ques-
tions with regard to Midiyanto's* gendèr *playing. Following the
recording beyond the transcribed portion, try to listen for repetition and
variation in the patterns played by Heri and Midiyanto. Note that they
always coincide with the 1 and the 6 in the middle and at the end of
the* balungan*.*

Musicians have far more choices when playing elaborating instruments than they do when seated at any of the other gamelan instruments.
What guides and constrains them? Musicians and scholars have tried
to articulate the underlying sense of the melodic flow of a piece. In
chapter 3, I noted that the idea of an unrevealed essence is prevalent in
such explanations. The issue is too complex for the scope of the present

book but is taken up at length in a study of magisterial scope by Marc Perlman (2004), who analyzes these accounts under the rubric of implicit melody. Here it will suffice to point once again both to the principle of convergence at *sèlèh* and to the importance of melodic register. For a given passage in a piece, there is usually consensus on the general melodic path that the musicians should take. The precise details of how they move along that path, however, depend on their individual choices. Oral formulaic theory, developed by Milman Parry and Albert Lord to explain how Yugoslav bards could sing enormously long oral poems, offers a useful explanatory tool here (Lord 2000). It presumes a structure with well-defined "slots" into which the performer can fit appropriate patterns. The "slots" in Javanese gamelan are defined by the structure of the piece (tending to be four beats in length), the goal tones, the mode, and the melodic register.

Musicians trained in the state arts schools (mentioned in chapter 4) usually have explicit, highly systematic knowledge of these matters. They often consider village musicians to be more instinctive because they do not have as extensive a vocabulary to talk about how they play. The Javanese term *naluri*—meaning instinct, heart, and ancient custom (among other things)—is sometimes applied to such musicians. This contrast between urban and village musicians is one of several binary oppositions that are fundamental to Javanese discourse on music. In lessons, interviews, and informal conversations, I constantly found musicians contrasting court and village styles, repertoires, and musicians. Some conflate this with a distinction between male and female styles of *gendèr* playing, an issue explored by scholars such as Sarah Weiss (2006) and Marc Perlman (1998).

The lines are rarely as clearly drawn in practice as they are in discourse about that practice. For instance, both Midiyanto and Heri Purwanto were born in villages in the rural area of Wonogiri, but each one studied at government schools for the performing arts in Solo, layering an academic court-centered knowledge over their early basis in village practice. Furthermore, both have siblings who have also studied in Solo. With numerous village musicians studying at the conservatory and academy, these distinctions are likely to continue to blur. The academy not only has continued court practices but has sponsored research and teaching of village practices as well. *Wayang kulit* is the area in which village practices are most valued and prevalent in the academy. This is the subject of the next two chapters, which outline the characteristics of the shadow play (chapter 6) and its musical aspects (chapter 7).

Shadows and Tales

WAYANG IN PANGKAH VILLAGE

One Saturday night in 1993, I watched the monthly live broadcast of *wayang kulit* (shadow play) at the government radio station in Solo. I did not stay until the end, returning home at 3:30 A.M. because I planned to see another all-night performance the following day in the region of Wonogiri, to the south of Solo. After a few hours of sleep, I dragged myself and my recording equipment to the station to catch a bus heading out of town. I hoped to make it to Midiyanto's village of Eromoko before he and his father left home with their musicians and instruments to perform at another, more distant village. They were gone by the time I reached Eromoko, but a young member of the family took me on his motorbike over little paths through the fields, video tripod, equipment bags, and all. We crossed a narrow body of water on a small ferry—a raft that could be propelled back and forth by pulling on a rope that stretched from one bank to the other. Another stretch of dirt paths brought us at last to Pangkah, a village set among dry upland fields rather than the wet rice fields of the lower lands around Solo and Yogya.

Pangkah lies close to the shore of a lake, enlarged enormously by the Indonesian government in the late 1970s to become the Gajah Mungkur reservoir. The lake flooded over 50 villages, forcing their inhabitants to move to other parts of Indonesia such as southern Sumatra. This was part of Indonesia's massive transmigration project that moved people out of the crowded areas of Java and Bali to less populated islands. Midiyanto remembers childhood friends uprooted by this calamity. Although far from their native area, these migrants have maintained connections and have invited Midiyanto to perform for his former neighbors in their new homes in Sumatra.

We arrived in Pangkah not too long after the performers because they had to take a winding road around the many long arms of the lake, their truckload of instruments and vans of musicians being too large and heavy for the back roads and ferry. The performance venue was the home of a *kyai*, a widely respected spiritual leader. Midiyanto's father, the shadow master Ki Sutino Hardokocarito, had a long-standing agreement to perform *wayang* every year at this *kyai*'s house on the eve of the Javanese new year, the first day of the month of Sura. (As this is basically the Muslim lunar calendar, the first of Sura has no direct equivalent in the Christian calendar, falling on a different day each year). Because this was a particularly auspicious time and many believe that attending such an occasion will enhance their well-being during the coming year, the performance drew large crowds, not just from the village but also from the surrounding area. Some crossed the lake in small boats; others took dirt roads through the fields.

The house of the *kyai* was situated 20 or 30 feet back from the road, behind a carefully swept dirt yard. The carved and painted wood panels of the front wall had been removed to create a performance space that overlapped the boundary between house and yard. This is a common feature of older village houses. The instruments of the gamelan were neatly arranged from the edge of the yard into the middle of the main room of the house. A large canvas screen stretched on a wooden frame was erected in front of them, running across the middle of that room, with seats for guests behind it and on either side. Although the surroundings differed radically from the city house of a wealthy businessman, this setup was remarkably similar to the one described in chapter 1—recall that the glass doors at the front of that house also had been removed to accommodate the *wayang* screen that separated light from shadow and men from women. In Pangkah, however, audience seating was not segregated by gender. The seats in the interior of the house, on the shadow side of the screen, were for the most important guests; others sat on chairs to either side of the gamelan while the dirt courtyard was left open for anyone else. Without guards or a wall around the courtyard, no invitation was actually required to attend. This practice is far more common than the restricted entry described in chapter 1.

I arrived just in time to hear the musicians play their first piece, "Ladrang Wilujeng," which is commonly performed at the beginning of an event to ensure the safety of those present; *wilujeng* means health and well-being. The text, however, was the same one you heard in "Ladrang Sri Katon" in chapter 4. It is sung in many other pieces and has nothing particular to do with well-being. Such song texts serve to embellish and enrich rather than to convey meaning particular to a given piece.

As soon as they had finished playing "Ladrang Wilujeng," the musicians launched into an abbreviated version of the *talu*, the sequence of pieces that is played as an "overture" to virtually every *wayang* performance. As the afternoon *wayang* was to be short, the *talu*, too, was abbreviated.

> **ACTIVITY 6.1** *Listen again to CD track 21 for a similar version of the* talu, *performed by many of the same musicians when I made the recordings for this book seven years later in Eromoko. Follow the notation for that piece (see figure 6.1), noting changes of irama and other contrasts as the musicians proceed through the sequence of pieces. In particular, you should note the intensification as the various types of colotomic gongs sound more frequently in each successive piece (you can see this in the notation). If you have been to operas or musicals, think about how this sequence compares to overtures you have heard in those contexts.*

I was intrigued to see that the *dhalang* was Ki Sutino's youngest son, Hendro, a teenager who had been studying at the performing arts high school in Solo. This was to be his formal debut. Ki Sutino and the host sat on chairs at the side of the gamelan, waiting to see how he would do. There was little point in sitting inside the house on the other side of the screen as it was still broad daylight and the lamp had not been lit to cast sharp shadows of the puppets on the screen. While the musicians played, the *dhalang* made his final preparations. He sat beneath the unlit lamp, facing the center of the screen.

Midiyanto gestured to me to play the *gambang* to the right of the *dhalang* as no one else was playing it. This afforded me a clear view of the *dhalang*'s every move and a chance to participate in the music. Over the course of the next one and a half hours, we made our way through a highly abbreviated shadow play. The performance was a success as Hendro demonstrated his abilities in the many areas of competence expected of a *dhalang*. He was stronger in some areas (such as puppet movement) than in others (such as singing), but the musicians and the few people watching clearly enjoyed his efforts.

The musicians were invited to a house across the road for a meal. This was my first chance to speak with the ones who had stayed with me and played gamelan in Berkeley two years earlier on their way to a summer residency at the Smithsonian Institution in Washington, D.C.

A. "Ladrang Sri Katon"

```
          - + -        - + -
[: .2.1 .2.6      .5.6 .5.3
     )      (        )      (
   .2.1 .2.6      .i.6 .5.3
     )      (        )      (
   .2.1 .2.6      .2.1 .2.6
     )      (        )      (
   .3.6 .3.(2)     .2.1 .2.(6) :]
                ⇗
                B
```

B. "Ketawang Suksma Ilang" (begins at 3:26)

```
   - + -  - + -  - + -  - + -
   ..26   1232   6123   653(2)
   33..   3353   6165   i65(3)
            (      )
   ..35   6356   3561   321(6)
            (      )      )
   ii..   3216   356i   321(6)
            (      )      )
   33..   6532   6123   653(2)  ⇒C
```

C. "Ayak-ayakan Manyura" (begins at 5:48)

```
   +      +      +      +       +      +
   ( 3 )  ((2))  ((2))  ((2))   (1)    ((6))
   +  +   + +    + +    + +     + +    +
    · 3    · 2    · 3    · 5     · 2    · 2
   ( 5 )  (3)    (5)    ((1))   ((2))  (32)
   +  +   + +    + +    + +     + +
   2 3 2  2 3    3 5    3 5     3 5    3 5 3
          (2 1)  (2 1)  (2 1)   (2 1)
   2 3 2  2 3 2  2 3 2  2 3 2   2 3 2
   (6)    (6)    (6)    (6)     ⇗D
[: 5 3 5  5 3 5  5 3 5  5 3 5   5 3 5    5 3 5 :]
```

100

D. "Srepegan Manyura" (begins at 6:39)

```
    +  +   +   +    +    +    +    +    +
   ( (  ( (   ( (   (    (   ( (   (   ( (
 3  2  [: 3  2  3   5    3   3  2  3   1
(3 2)    (2 1)  (3 2)   ((3 2)  ((3 2)  ((3 1)
    2  1  3     2    5    6    i    6
   (2 1) (3 2) (5 6) (3 1)
    i  6  5     3    6    5    3    2
   (i 6) (3 5) (3 5) (3 2)                    E  ⇑
                                              :]
```

E. "Sampak Manyura" (begins at 7:33)

```
 +x +x +x +x +x +x +x +x +x +x +x +x +x +x +x +x
[: 6 6 6 6 3 3 3 3 3 2 2 2 2 2 2 2 ((
   2 2 2 2 3 3 3 3 1 1 1 1 (1)
   1 1 1 1 2 2 2 2 6 6 6 6 (6)
   3 3 3 2 2 2 2 (2)  6 6 6 6 6 :]  §
                                6 6 6 6 6 6 5 3 (2)
```

§ *suwuk:*   ⇑ = transition to next piece

Key: [: :] = repeated section

FIGURE 6.1 *A short version of the wayang overture called "Talu" or "Patalon." The colotomic pattern notated in the first line of each section continues throughout that section.*

101

After smiles and greetings, we dressed in formal performance attire and returned to the performance area just as it grew dark. Guests had already started to arrive and be shown to the chairs inside the house while recorded music blared from two large stacks of speakers standing at the sides of the opening in the front wall. A few vendors had arrived to sell snacks and cheap toys in the street.

As a preface to the full performance, the musicians played a very loud, fast *ladrang*. They followed this with a slower, softer one that gave the female singers an opportunity to warm up their voices before performing the full version of the *talu*, the "overture" that had been played in abbreviated form a few hours earlier.

JAVANESE SHADOW PLAYS

Javanese audiences have been experiencing shadow plays for centuries, and gamelan music of some sort has been an essential component of these performances. This makes it an ancient art form, but that adjective (a favorite of impresarios and public relations people) obscures the constant changes in *wayang* as performers adapt it to maintain its contemporary relevancy and to draw audiences. In the course of the twentieth century alone, *wayang* (and its music) underwent substantial changes, enabling it to remain popular despite competition from theater, film, and television.

Wayang serves as entertainment: it can be wildly funny, deeply moving, full of engrossing action, and sensuously pleasant to the ears. At the same time, it is a means of ritual celebration and a form of education. *Wayang* is considered by many to be the ultimate expression of Javanese culture, to embody the essence of Javanese philosophy. It can convey other messages as well. In the past, Javanese aristocrats doubtless favored the *wayang* in part because its characteristic emphasis on kings and feudalism served to reinforce their hierarchical view of social order and their own places in that order. In more recent times, Indonesia's first president, Sukarno, was likened to a puppeteer, and political factions as varied as the Indonesian Communist Party and President Suharto's repressive military regime utilized *wayang* as an effective vehicle for propaganda.

Of all the many people involved in any *wayang* performance, the most important is the *dhalang*, the shadow master who tells the story, manipulates the puppets, speaks all the dialogue, and cues the gamelan to provide the music appropriate to each part of the performance. The *dhalang* is respected, even revered. A repository of traditional knowledge, he (infrequently she) has the power to bring the two-dimensional rawhide puppets to life. Some *dhalangs*, particularly older ones, are also healers who possess spiritual power. A special type of short exorcistic *wayang* can only be performed by such a *dhalang*. It is a measure of the importance of the figure of the *dhalang* in Javanese culture that the mastermind behind a political plot is said to be the *dhalang*; the noun has even been made into a verb in Indonesian to indicate behind-the-scenes manipulation.

A full *wayang* performance is a display of invention, recall, performative power, and sheer endurance. Typically lasting from 8 or 9 P.M. until 5 or 6 A.M., the show requires almost constant activity on the part of the *dhalang*. He may take a few moments to smoke or drink tea while the gamelan plays, but he remains seated throughout and eats nothing. Puppet manipulation requires both great dexterity to move the rods controlling the arms of one or two puppets in a nuanced manner and strength to hold large puppets at arm's length. The narration, dialogue, and numerous requisite songs all make demands on the *dhalang*'s voice. Consider, too, that he might have traveled several hours to reach the performance site and will probably have spent a few hours with the host of the event prior to mounting the stage. Finally, add to this the fact that a successful *dhalang* may perform as frequently as 25 times in a month during certain portions of the year. Being a *dhalang* is certainly one of the most demanding professions imaginable.

A *dhalang* works from memory as he calls up the various characters with their individual personalities and histories, their complex relationships with one another. He must know the plots of many episodes, the numerous names borne by some of the main characters, and the characteristic narrative phrases and intricacies of formal address appropriate to a scene involving kings, princes, generals, servants, and perhaps a visiting god or ogre. He must also know a large musical repertoire in ways that I will discuss in the next chapter. All of these resources are worked into a performance that almost invariably follows a highly conventionalized dramatic structure. But the *dhalang* also invents. He elaborates on the memorized bits and the conventions by creating dialogues, new plot twists, and verbal, visual, and musical humor. Very few *wayang* performances are extensively scripted; fewer still depart radically from accepted conventions, although there has been considerable variation and innovation recently.

With all of these demands, it should come as no surprise that many years of training are required to become a full-fledged *dhalang*. Almost every *dhalang* is born into a family of *dhalangs* and begins to absorb the complex body of knowledge as a little child. He is likely to play in the gamelan accompanying his father, uncle, or older brother. He may also assist with the puppets, sitting to the right or left of the *dhalang* and observing at close range. He may go on to train at a performing arts high school or college to polish and extend the knowledge gained at home. It is not unusual for youngsters to perform while still in training. I have seen promising performances by children ages 10 or 11, but these were brief excerpts and usually showed strength in one area, such as puppet manipulation or memorized narration, while others, such as singing, remained to be developed. A full performance is truly demanding, and the *dhalang*'s pay reflects this—for one show he may earn the equivalent of hundreds or even thousands of dollars while his musicians earn a few dollars.

Whenever possible, a *dhalang* works with a steady group of musicians and his own gamelan instruments. He knows the musicians' capabilities and the tuning of the gamelan while the musicians know his cues and habits. This mutual familiarity enables better performances because rehearsal for a full performance is relatively uncommon. Certain segments may be worked out or a new composition or musical arrangement may be learned in rehearsal, but many aspects of a show are crafted on the spot in the course of performance. This improvisation is possible because of the extensive body of dramatic and musical conventions that has evolved and is widely shared. These conventions become even more important when a *dhalang* performs with someone else's gamelan or an unfamiliar group of musicians. In such cases, a *dhalang* will always try to bring at least a few musicians familiar with his personal style to lead the group, but the other musicians will only be able to follow if they share those conventions.

THE STORIES AND THE TELLING: THE MAIN ELEMENTS

Physical Setup. To stage a *wayang*, one needs a large cloth screen stretched taut over a wooden frame. The screen is made of white cotton with a dark-colored opaque border. Along the bottom of the screen are tied the trunks of banana trees in two layers. Readily available virtually everywhere, the banana tree offers a firm but spongy support into which the *dhalang* can easily stick his puppets. The two layers allow a hierarchical placement, with more important figures standing on the upper layer. The banana trunks extend out to either side of the screen where they support a tightly packed display of the puppets that

FIGURE 6.2 Wayang kulit *performance with oil lamp. Mangkunagaran Palace,* *1983. (Photo by Ben Brinner.)*

will not be used in that evening's performance, all neatly arranged in order of ascending height to create an imposing display (see figure 6.2; note that a wooden rack was used to hold the flanking puppets in this performance). Characters belonging to the "good" side are arranged on the *dhalang*'s right while those from the "bad" side are on his left. Good and bad are relative terms here, clear-cut in some stories but complicated in others.

Hanging from the top center of the screen's frame is a lamp with which the *dhalang* casts shadows. Electric lights have almost completely replaced the older coconut oil lamp, with its flickering flame. The two shows I witnessed with an oil lamp were self-consciously traditional reenactments at the Mangkunagaran palace, commissioned by a group of Japanese *wayang* aficionados. The *dhalang* sits beneath and just behind this lamp. Using the space between the lamp and the screen, he can cast shadows over any part of the screen and can control with great precision the size and sharpness of the shadow. Pressed up against the screen, every detail of a puppet's carving is clearly outlined; held back and up to the left or right, a puppet's shadow grows greatly as its edges

FIGURE 6.3 Wayang *arranged for an audience scene. From left to right: King Baladewa, the white monkey Hanoman, the gods Narada and Guru (Shiva) and the* kayon, *which can symbolize a throne, a palace, a mountain, a tree, and even the wind. It also serves as a "curtain" demarcating the boundary between scenes.* (Photo by Ben Brinner.)

become more vague and it seems to float in the air. Although everything is calculated to create and manipulate these shadows, many enjoy watching from the *dhalang*'s side of the screen. In some cases, the screen is pressed right against a wall; there is no shadow side.

All of these elements are invested with symbolism. According to one interpretation, the banana logs are the earth, the screen is the universe, the lamp is the sun, and the *dhalang* is God. The *kayon* puppet (also called *gunungan*) that occupies the center of the screen at the beginning, the end, and every major juncture in the course of the play (on the right in figure 6.3) represents both a mountain (*gunung*) and a forest or tree (*kayu*), central elements in animistic belief systems that predate the advent of Hinduism, Buddhism, Islam, and Christianity in Java.

The *kayon* and all the other puppets are cut from rawhide using special chisels. The hair and clothing are often ornate filigree. A thin piece of water buffalo horn snakes down from the head of the puppet to a sharp handle that the *dhalang* can plunge into the banana log at the foot of the screen. One or two smaller handles attach to the puppet's hands to enable the *dhalang* to manipulate its arms, which are articulated at the shoulder and often at the elbow, too. Although the primary purpose of the puppets is to cast shadows, they are ornately painted. This is seen by anyone sitting on the *dhalang*'s side of the screen; a faint glimmer of the color is often visible on the shadow side as well.

To the *dhalang*'s left is a large wooden box that serves as the storage case for the puppets, as a percussion instrument for sound effects and cues, and as a support for the *kepyak* (a set of overlapping bronze plates that the *dhalang* also uses for sound effects and cues). He sounds the box and the *kepyak* with a specially shaped wooden mallet held in the left hand or between the toes of the right foot. To the *dhalang*'s right is the lid of the box on which he can place puppets that he is likely to use. One or two assistants help keep the puppets in order and ready for use at an instant's notice. The gamelan is arranged behind the *dhalang* and often to his left and right as well. I will discuss the logic of that layout presently.

Plots and Plot Sources.   In Central Java, the vast majority of *wayang* performances present episodes from either the Mahabharata or the Ramayana, two lengthy tales that were brought from India to Java, Bali, and other parts of Southeast Asia over 1,000 years ago. Each has been transmitted in both written and oral forms, generating numerous variants which are all recognizably related to their Indian antecedents but which differ from them in various ways. The variants differ from each other, too, of course. There is no undisputed correct version of either the Mahabharata or the Ramayana. In addition to these two primary sources, indigenous Javanese stories about the medieval prince Panji and other stories have been recounted in various forms of puppet play as well as in theater with human actors.

The Ramayana features Prince Rama, wandering in exile in a forest with his wife, Sita, and his brother, Laksmana. Sita is coveted by a coarse ogre, Rahwana, invincible king of Alengka. Rahwana tricks Rama into leaving his wife's side to pursue a golden deer; when Laksmana goes to search for his brother who has failed to return, Rahwana swoops down and flies off with Sita. A large bird, a *garuda*, tries to rescue Sita but fails. Wounded by Rahwana, he falls to the ground where Rama and Laksmana learn from him of Sita's capture. Rama becomes involved in a conflict between the monkey king Subali and his brother, Sugriwa. By helping Sugriwa to become king, Rama gains his aid. With the particular assistance of the monkey Hanuman (see figure 6.3), son of the god of the wind, Rama eventually succeeds in finding Sita and rescuing her after defeating Rahwana and his army of ogres.

While it is possible to compress the essence of the story into a single performance, this is mostly done in dance dramas for tourists and occurs rarely in *wayang kulit*. The one attempt I saw was not well received by the audience. It is common practice to take one episode and extend it over an entire night. A particularly popular episode recounts Hanuman's mission to find the captive Sita and tell her that Rama is coming to rescue her. The audience knows it in great detail yet delights in the way a particular *dhalang* presents it.

The Mahabharata is far more extensive than the Ramayana, with hundreds of characters and numerous episodes stretching in a nonlinear fashion over several generations. At the heart of this complex of stories is the rivalry for the throne of Astina, which is disputed by two sets of cousins: the 5 righteous Pandawa brothers versus their treacherous cousins, the 100 Kurawa. While the majority of performances probably deal directly with these characters, many episodes precede their births and a few follow their deaths. Hanging over the entire Mahabharata is the climactic war, the Bharatayudha, which cannot be averted. In this war, the two sets of warring cousins will marshal their allies to shed enormous amounts of blood. Audiences know that certain characters are fated to fight each other to the death in that war; sometimes the characters know it, too.

Despite their Indian origins and the dominance of Islam in Java for many centuries, these characters are widely perceived as ancestors of modern Javanese. The two epic cycles are viewed as connected by particular characters. For instance, the monkey Hanuman from the Ramayana (see figure 6.3) is thought to be the brother of Bima (see figure 6.4), the strongest of the Pandawa brothers from the Mahabharata, because they are both sons of the god Bayu.

The main plots are well known. A *dhalang* strays from these at his peril; however, it is common practice to create subsidiary tales that branch off from the main trunk of stories handed down through the generations. These so-called branch stories still make use of the traditional characters but put them in new situations. The *dhalang* can invent new characters, but they must be in keeping with the existing stories and conventions. He must still take into account the overall narrative of the Mahabharata. In this way, *wayang* performance offers opportunities for alteration and improvisation through oral formulaity, being up-to-date while maintaining tradition and teaching the younger generations.

Characters and Character Types.   Many Javanese have extensive knowledge of the main characters of the *wayang* world. They know them as individuals and in a web of relations to other characters, linked through kinship, fealty, enmity, or some other relationship. They know their moral character—their honesty or deceptiveness, bravery or

FIGURE 6.4 *Opponents in the play "Brajadenta Balela." On the left stands Gathutkaca, king of Pringgandani (note his crown), flanked by his parents, Bima and the ogress Arimbi. Facing them are Betari Durga, goddess of the dead, and Brajadenta, Gathutkaca's ogre uncle and rebellious Prime Minister. Note the extreme differences in size. Brajadenta's large round eyes, fangs, and beard represent extreme coarseness.* (Photo by Ben Brinner.)

cowardice, humility or arrogance—and their individual histories. People also recognize the different categories of characters: gods and goddesses, kings and queens, knights, sages, servants, ogres, animals, and so on.

These categories intersect with many dimensions of variation in character. Most important is the dichotomy between *alus* and *kasar* (refined and coarse, respectively), a contrast fundamental to Javanese thought and social mores. Arjuna, one of the Pandawas, epitomizes the *alus* ideal, refined in every respect (see figure 6.5). He battles ogres who are his polar opposite, coarse to the bone. Other figures stand somewhere between these extremes.

Humility and arrogance as well as bravery and cowardice are encoded in a complex iconography, developed over centuries, which also represents a puppet's status. Information about a character can be read from the shape of the eye (varying from round to narrow), the angle of the head, the amount of adornment on the body, even the color of the face (see figure 6.5). Arjuna and his brother Bima are both warrior princes, but Arjuna's slight frame, narrow eyes, nose shape, and lack of facial hair indicate his refinement while Bima's stride, his large body and features, his round eyes, his protruding nose and beard are all signs of a strong, almost coarse male. Bima is *gagah*, strong rather than coarse

FIGURE 6.5 *The forest demon Cakil (left) holds a dagger as he confronts Arjuna (center). Arjuna's humility is evident in his downcast gaze and lack of bodily ornaments. His long, narrow eye symbolizes refinement and his black face restraint. Cakil is Arjuna's opposite in character and behavior as well as looks—note his fangs, widespread legs, beard, and adornments. In every play he confronts Arjuna (or another hero) early in the second act (pathet) and inevitably is killed. Behind Arjuna stand the punakawan, his servant-companions: Semar, a disgraced god, and his sons Garèng and Petruk, who squabble constantly. They speak colloquial Javanese and are the dhalang's main vehicle for comedy. (Photo by Ben Brinner.)*

like the ogres. Arjuna's downcast gaze shows his humility. By contrast, Queen Banowati looks straight ahead because she is less humble (see figure 6.6). Such features are highly conventionalized throughout a region and transcend the personal style of individual puppet makers, which manifests only in subtle details.

A reasonably complete set of puppets may number over 300 and will include props such as arrows, spears, and other weapons. For certain characters such as Arjuna, a different puppet is needed for each stage in the character's life. In addition to numerous specifically named puppets, there are generic ones that represent a character type rather than a specific character.

ACTIVITY 6.2 *Think of a television drama or movie that you know well. Based on the photos of puppets and my explanation of Javanese wayang, how would you depict the characters?*

FIGURE 6.6 *King Duryudana of Astina, eldest of the one hundred Kurawa broth-ers, faces his wife, Queen Banowati, whose boldness is evident in her direct gaze. She is accompanied by her servants, a mother and her daughter, who provide comic relief early in the performance. The king is accompanied by Sangkuni, his prime minister. (Photo by Ben Brinner.)*

Language and Voice. The language of *wayang,* a mix of special the-atrical language with modern Javanese, older Javanese, and ancient Indian Sanskrit, is exceptionally rich and varied. It deserves extensive treatment in its own right. A brief survey of the main types of speech acts will have to suffice here. The three plays translated in Brandon's *On Thrones of Gold* (1970) give a sense of the range of expression. (Note, however, that these are translations not of live performances but of scripts published for pedagogical purposes.)

Narration can range from a single sentence announcing a change of place to a lengthy passage that describes elaborately the wealth of a kingdom and expounds on the king's lineage and the meanings of his many names. These passages tend to be highly formulaic. They are flexible enough to accommodate various characters, places, and situa-tions but fixed enough to be instantly recognizable as *wayang* narration even when taken completely out of context. A good *dhalang* can elabo-rate endlessly and smoothly on this stock of phrases. One who is still learning can get by with memorizing a few narrative runs; if his puppet movement is good, his jokes funny, or his singing beautiful, the audi-ence may forgive less florid and varied narration.

Dialogue ranges from highly formulaic exchanges of greetings, farewells, and battle challenges to more spontaneous clowning and philosophical disquisitions. The principle of appropriateness operates here just as it does in so many aspects of Javanese music. "According to established practice," writes the *dhalang* Probohardjono, "*antawacana* [dialogue] must be in accord with the different emotions, moods, and facial features of the characters" (1984: 492). The *dhalang* must master a range of speaking styles linked to particular characters and character types and distinguished by linguistic register, pitch register, vocal timbre, and intonation patterns. The term *linguistic register* refers to the different levels of formality in Javanese language, distinguished mainly by vocabulary. Courtly language and special stage expressions further complicate the picture. At all times the *dhalang* must remember the relative status of the characters on stage so that the characters use the appropriate speech levels as they talk to one another.

ACTIVITY 6.3 *Listen to CD track 31 to hear Midiyanto perform the voices of various well-known* wayang *characters Arjuna, Cakil (0:07), Bima (0:13), Kresna (0:21), Semar (0:29), Banowati (0:45), Gathutkaca (0:51), and Brajadenta (0:58). Midiyanto produced these examples at a moment's notice, not in the context of a performance, so this is not a continuous dialogue. He has each character speak a typical formulaic greeting or challenge. In a paragraph contrast two of these voices in terms of aspects such as register, contour, speed, and vocal quality. You can see each of these characters except Kresna in figures 6.3 to 6.6. Do you think the voices match the images?*

Choose a TV show and write a brief analysis of the speech patterns of contrasting characters. The vocal patterns in wayang *differ greatly from those of most TV shows. Do you find similarities in the parameters that are being manipulated to differentiate characters?*

Movement Patterns. A good *dhalang* captivates the audience in many ways, not least through manipulation of the puppets. Fighting, dancing, riding a horse—all are opportunities to animate the characters and transcend the apparent limitations of two-dimensional screen and puppets. Like other aspects of *wayang*, puppet movement is both conventionalized and open to variations of personal style. Some *dhalangs* have achieved fame through their ability to manipulate several puppets at once. All the puppets belonging to a character type usually share a particular style of movement. Some characters are immediately recognizable for their idiosyncratic ways of moving: Gathutkaca, a popular prince, flies through the air (see figure 6.4); the clown-servant Garèng has a characteristic limp (see figure 6.5); and Dursasana, a particularly large and coarse member of the 100 Kurawa brothers, has difficulty standing still. A good *dhalang* will maintain these idiosyncrasies and play them against each other. The forest demon Cakil, who challenges the protagonist in the middle of virtually every performance, moves rapidly and excessively while his opponent, often a highly refined warrior such as Arjuna (see figure 6.5), barely needs to move a muscle in order to defeat him (imagine a diminutive Tai Chi master against a large flailing boxer). The challenge here is to convey—with one hand—the inner power of a refined warrior through minimal movement while moving the demon in a frenzied fashion with the other. Listen for this contrast between restraint and wildness in the voices of Arjuna and Cakil (CD track 31).

Dramatic Structure: Schemata of Various Sizes. Mastery of plot, characters, narration, dialogue, and puppet manipulation would be useless without a good understanding of how to structure a performance. Javanese *wayang* theory is quite explicit in this area, and practice is not too distant from theory in most cases. Among the many conventions shaping performance in Central Java, the large-scale structure or schema of a *wayang* is one of the most important; even very short *wayang* performances will maintain traces of this structure. It consists of three major divisions, called *pathet* (roughly equivalent to an act in a play), each linked to a particular musical mode, which is also called *pathet*. Each act has characteristic content.

The first *pathet* is more serious and slower-moving than the others, beginning in a royal court where some challenge or problem arises and is discussed. There is considerable narrative redundancy as the problem discussed in the first scene is retold to other characters in the second and third. This adds to the formality of the occasion and also allows audience members to catch up if they arrive late or tune out for a while. Usually a character is sent off on a mission, often accompanied by an army. Several changes of location are likely, and so is an inconclusive battle in which no one is killed.

The protagonist often does not appear until the second *pathet*, where he is commonly first seen in the mountains or a forest, meditating or studying with a wise hermit. He is accompanied by three or four servants (*punakawan*, see figure 6.5) who entertain the audience mightily with their antics. The servants speak in everyday language (unlike the other characters), connecting with the audience in a much more immediate way. A large portion of the second act may be devoted to musical entertainment as the servants call on the gamelan to perform various songs. Eventually the drama gets under way again and the protagonist sets out on a mission, inevitably encountering demons or ogres in the forest and proving his prowess by defeating them. The third *pathet* is generally the most action-packed, with frequent extensive battles that foreground puppet manipulation and fast, loud gamelan music. The problem is resolved, often just about the time the sun rises on a new day.

At the performance in Pangkah, Ki Sutino followed this structure. Due to the seriousness of the occasion—the beginning of a new year— he devoted more time than usual to philosophical matters in the first *pathet*, so the second one did not start until nearly 1 A.M., unusually late. He finished the show well after sunrise. The audience came and went during the night, surging in the early hours and then waning in the middle. From about 4 A.M. on, I noticed mothers bringing their freshly scrubbed children to see the end of the show.

CONCLUSION

The tools of oral formulaic theory, mentioned in connection with elaborating parts in chapter 5, have been applied to oral narratives in most parts of the world. They apply here, too (see A. L. Becker 1979), just as they do in the related Balinese and Malay shadow theater (see Gold 2005: 87 and Sweeney 1980: 41–62, respectively). To perform a given plot, the *dhalang* draws on a highly varied but clearly ordered body of knowledge that includes plot structures, scene types and structures, character types, specific characters, voices, levels of speech, and formulaic expressions of many sorts. Formulaity applies not only to language but to patterns of puppet manipulation and to musical elements of the show. With these tools, a *dhalang* and his troupe of musicians can perform for an entire night without prior rehearsal. To enthrall the audience, the *dhalang* must go beyond the formulaic, but he cannot abandon it without risking the coherence of the performance.

These resources have been codified in oral tradition, in books, and in teaching curricula aimed at training aspiring puppeteers. Schools for training *dhalang*s were established in both Yogyakarta and Surakarta under the aegis of royal courts in the decades preceding World War II. Since the 1950s, training in *wayang* has also spread and been further developed in secondary and tertiary performing arts schools. This has spurred considerable efforts to document and codify *wayang* practices, including publication of sample scripts and notation of musical accompaniment. Yet considerable flexibility persists. Being born into a *dhalang*'s family remains a nearly inescapable prerequisite for success. Performers I have asked have agreed that formal education simply is not sufficient for success as a *dhalang*; there is so much to know that learning by osmosis in early childhood seems to be a major component in a *dhalang*'s formation. Formal training is a powerful supplement to that basis, not a replacement for it.

Scripting parts of a performance has become more common in recent years. This enabled Ki Tristuti Rahmadi, an important *dhalang* who was imprisoned by the Indonesian government for many years due to his connections to the Indonesian Communist Party, to continue to work in *wayang* after his release, although he was forbidden to perform. His fame was such that other *dhalangs* turned to him for advice and texts that they could incorporate into their performances. Performing an entire play from a script, however, remains the mark of an amateur. One exception to this generalization is some experimental shows that are fully scripted either because they involve several *dhalangs* who must coordinate their work or because they are so highly abbreviated that every word counts. Virtually every other performance is improvised in the sense that it is assembled on the spot, with relatively little prior rehearsal and with many decisions made in the course of performance. Thus tremendous flexibility is required of the *dhalang* and the musicians; also needed is a large stock of knowledge from which to draw in the course of performance.

The imprisonment of Ki Tristuti is evidence of a *dhalang*'s power. A good *dhalang* captivates the audience and manipulates its expectations and mood. This puts him (or her) in a privileged position to impart information, to put across a particular slant on contemporary events. The Indonesian Communist Party realized this potential in the years prior to its violent suppression by the military in 1965. Many of the performers associated with it were killed or imprisoned. The government also took advantage of *dhalangs* as a conduit for advancing its own agendas. The fact that political machinations are central to many *wayang* plots only enhances the effectiveness of the medium.

Through all the innovations that have occurred in *wayang* over the years, the sense that performers' choices ought to be appropriate both to context and to a range of other constraints continues. Prince Arjuna will always be a refined warrior, and this requires speaking and moving in certain ways and not in others. His servant Petruk will always be coarse and funny (see figure 6.5). There is no possibility of confusing the two, yet there is still considerable scope to each character.

Innovations that have sparked controversy involve the aesthetic balance among the contrasting elements of a *wayang* performance. Some complain, for instance, that comic scenes have displaced too much of the serious philosophical teachings or that action scenes have become too prominent. Here again, appropriateness is held up as a standard; some find extensive clowning in the first act inappropriate to the overall ethos of that act. One expects shifting focus—at times humor, sometimes pure musical enjoyment, at other times a solemn feeling of awe at the grandeur of the scene or the heroic stance of a character. There should be something for everyone. It boils down to a question of balance.

ACTIVITY 6.4 *Choose a TV show that you know well and write an essay analyzing it in terms of dramatic structure and characters you consider highly conventionalized. Do the episodes share a common structure? Have you encountered that structure (or parts of it) in other shows? What sort of character types does the show use? List the means by which one type is distinguished from another. Is music used to delineate the structure or the character types?*

Of course, *wayang kulit* differs in crucial ways from a sitcom. In sheer length, in pacing, in number of subplots, and in variety of characters, it dwarfs a one-hour TV show. But there is also the immediacy of the experience, the food and conversation, with hawkers and sometimes gambling at the margins of the performance area, not to mention the overwhelmingly male audience. All of these are part of the *wayang* experience, though they may not all be present at every performance. The essential component that cannot be replaced is music, created live, in the moment, in close interaction with the *dhalang*. The numerous dramatic and musical possibilities require flexibility and a complex set of conventions by which to make appropriate choices. Nowhere is the interconnnectedness of the arts more apparent in Javanese culture. This is the subject of the next chapter.

CHAPTER 7

Music for Motion and Emotion—*Wayang Kulit*

"BRAJADENTA BALELA"

I first met Ki Sutino Hardokocarito (introduced at the beginning of chapter 6) when Midiyanto brought a small *wayang kulit* troupe to the United States in 1991 for a two-month residency at the Smithsonian in Washington, D.C. While there, they recorded *Shadow Music of Java* (see Resources). Most of the musicians who accompanied Ki Sutino later took part in the *wayang* described in chapter 6 and participated in the recordings for this book.

On the way to Washington, the group stopped in Berkeley to perform a *wayang*. A few experienced players from the University of California at Berkeley's gamelan group supplemented the eight musicians from Java. We held a couple of rehearsals to solidify the group and work out a shortened version of an all-night play. The performance, lasting two and a half hours, was held in a church near the campus. I spoke to the audience before the show, showing them some of the puppets and telling them about the story since it would all be performed in Javanese. Such explanations would be entirely unnecessary in Java, of course, but it is not uncommon for local officials there to exploit the occasion of a *wayang* performance to make speeches.

The chosen story, "Brajadenta Balela," featured characters from the Mahabharata cycle. It concerned rivalry over the throne of an ogre kingdom ruled by Gathutkaca, son of Arimbi, an ogress, and Bima, the strongest of the five Pandawa brothers (see figure 6.4). Gathutkaca is almost as strong as his father and resembles him in appearance, but he also has the ability to fly. Bima had killed Arimbi's brother, the ogre king of Pringgadani. Most of the ogres accepted Gathutkaca as their new ruler, but Prime Minister Brajadenta, one of the dead king's brothers, rebelled (hence the title of the play).

At the end of the overture (CD track 21), the *dhalang* cued the musicians to begin a rather long piece, "Gendhing Kabor." This is a *gendhing gendèr*, meaning that the introduction is played on *gendèr* rather than *rebab*. Ki Sutino took the *kayon*, a very large puppet (on the right in figure 6.3), that he had placed in the center of the screen and twirled it, finally "planting" it on the far right, in the styrofoam that substituted for a banana log below the screen. Like a curtain in a theater, this *kayon* would be used throughout the play to mark every change of scene. He then brought the puppets on, their entrances timed to coincide with the *kenong* and gong strokes that marked the colotomic structure of the *gendhing*. He chose to begin the story not in the protagonist's home in Pringgadani but in the kingdom of Astina, initiating a different plot concerning the rivalry between cousins (Kurawas and Pandawas) that lies at the heart of the Mahabharata. Such layering of plots and places is typical of *wayang*.

The first scene centered on King Duryudana, eldest of the Kurawa brothers (see figure 6.6). He took his place to the *dhalang's* right, with his maidservants behind him. His teacher, his prime minister, and one of his many brothers entered, bowing to the king before being placed on the left, facing the king. When all the necessary puppets were on the screen, the *dhalang* cued the gamelan to play softly so that he could begin to tell the story, describing in a highly formulaic manner the king and his kingdom. He then cued the gamelan to resume playing at full volume and switch to a different piece. Another cue brought the piece to a close. Ki Sutino produced most of these cues by tapping the wooden puppet box with a mallet. He then sang the customary opening song. Its text, derived from the *Bharatayudha Kakawin*, a very old Javanese poem about the climactic war of the Mahabharata, is appropriate to this opening scene because it describes the splendor of the palace and the sleeping chamber of Duryudana's wife, Queen Banowati.

ACTIVITY 7.1 *The sequence I have just summarized is excerpted on CD track 32 (each fade out is a cut in the original). You will hear several radical changes in speed, volume, texture, melody, and drumming. Match the time codes for each musical change to the sequence described above.*

At the end of the song, the gamelan was finally silent, after nearly half an hour of music. The *dhalang* began to speak for the puppets, beginning with the formal exchange of greetings typical of such a meeting or audience scene. He then presented a problem: King Duryudana did not know how to respond to an invitation from his archrivals (and cousins), the Pandawas, to consecrate a new shrine. After some debate, the king decided to accept and ordered his prime minister to guard the kingdom in his absence.

To end the first scene, the *dhalang* cued "Srepeg Nem" by tapping a particular rhythm and moved the puppets off the screen in time to the music once again. This piece is typical of "walking music," played to accompany characters as they travel from place to place, do battle, or engage in other physical activity. With gongs struck very frequently, it offers the *dhalang* numerous opportunities to move puppets on and off the screen. The slow pace at the beginning of a scene need not be replicated at its end.

ACTIVITY 7.2 *Listen to CD track 33 while following the notation of "Srepeg Nem" in figure 7.1. Each sequence of accents tapped on the puppet box and played on the drums matches a puppet movement. The drummer, Pak Wakidi, switches between two drums: the* kendhang sabet, *a lower-pitched drum specific to* wayang, *and a* ciblon. *What else changes when he switches drums?*

To demarcate the boundary between scenes, the *dhalang* sang a short song accompanied by *gendèr* and then spoke a few words of narration to set the scene in the outer courtyard of the palace. Tapping the same rhythmic cue as before on the puppet box, he had the musicians play "Srepeg Nem" again as he brought out the puppets for the next scene. In the courtyard of the palace, the prime minister relayed orders to the king's brothers and officers, repeating some of the discussion from the first scene. This seeming redundancy is typical of *wayang* and would be greater in a full-length performance where another scene typically comes between these two, a scene in which the king recounts the meeting to his wife. Initiating the same story three times gives the *dhalang* a chance to cast the issue in a different light in each scene as the speakers and the context shift from the audience chamber to the inner palace to the outer courtyard. The character and pacing of each scene differ, too. The first is slowest and most serious, a good opportunity for the *dhalang* to incorporate Javanese philosophy. The scene with the queen involves her two servants, a scrawny old mother and her very large daughter (see figure 6.6). This is an excuse to interrupt the story with

235 [:6565 2353 5353 5235 i653 6532 ⊕3232 3565 :]   return to beginning of *srepeg*

ngelik   2121 3232   56i6 i6i6 2321 3265 3235

⊕ *suwuk*   3232 6532

Key: [: :] repeat the section between the brackets   ⊕ = point of transition to the *ngelik* section.

FIGURE 7.1   *"Srepeg Sléndro Nem." This gendhing lampah has an optional ngelik section, with a melody in the high register, that may be played once. In addition to the gongs indicated, the kethuk is played off the beat and the kenong is played twice as frequently, coinciding with the kethuk and the kempul.*

a comic interlude that has become quite extensive in recent years. The daughter aspires to be a dancer and singer, but her size and deep speaking voice (the *dhalang's*) would seem to preclude that. Yet when she opens her mouth to sing, it is the *pesindhèn's* voice that is heard. By contrast, the third scene foregrounds the rougher male characters of the prime minister and warriors.

After all this talking, it was time for some extended action. The *dhalang* cued a piece in *lancaran* form, calling for "Lancaran Singa Nebah" by working the title into his narration. The singers sang an introduction and the drummer cued the gamelan to begin the piece in *irama* 1 (CD track 34), not the fast *irama lancar* beginning that you heard in CD tracks 13, 19, and 26. In the course of the piece (which lasted nearly 15 minutes but could easily have lasted half an hour in a full performance), the drummer changed *irama* several times in accordance with the parade of puppets that crossed the screen. First, the characters left the courtyard scene: several of them crossed the screen individually, dancing and posturing to the music as the drummer changed rhythms to highlight each puppet's characteristic moves. He then accelerated to the most condensed *irama*. One of the king's brothers stood in the middle of the screen and gestured with his arms. A large puppet representing a whole army responded by marching across the screen. The drummer and *saron* players accompanied this with special rhythms (CD track 34, at 2:21). Another of the king's brothers came on with his horse, trying to mount it. This is a common comic moment that a *dhalang* can play in various ways. Once the warrior is mounted on his horse, the *dhalang* turns from comedy to a demonstration of dexterity, as both horse and rider are articulated puppets. The warrior's arms and the horse's head are movable. After showing the soldiers carrying out the king's orders, the *dhalang* brought on a puppet of a carriage pulled by horses and had King Duryudana and his traveling companions enter the carriage to set out on their journey while the musicians continued to play "Lancaran Singa Nebah." He tilted the *kayon* at one end of the screen to represent a mountain and drove the carriage up the slope.

ACTIVITY 7.3 *While following the notation in figure 7.2, listen to CD track 34 (which has been edited down from 15 minutes to 5, with excerpts taken from the beginning, middle, and end). Write down the time code for each change in* irama. *Listen to the changes in elaboration. Can you hear the special drumming and*

rhythm played when the army puppet passes across the screen (2:21 to 2:38)? When do you hear the saron *players briefly alter the melody? At the end, the drummer plays the* suwuk *pattern notated in figure 2.6. Can you hear it?*

Once again the *dhalang* marked a change of scene by singing a song and placing the *kayon* in the center of the screen. With a sentence or two of narration, he brought the audience to a new portion of the play. In *wayang kulit*'s conventional structure, this scene is usually set in a foreign kingdom, often populated by ogres or other nonhumans. In this case it was Pringgadani, the ogre kingdom ruled by Gathutkaca. The scene began in a manner very similar to that of the first scene of the play. The *dhalang* cued the musicians to begin a piece (this time by alluding to its name in his narration) and brought the characters onto the screen timed to the strokes of *kenong* and gong. When the scene was set, he tapped out a rhythm on the puppet box to cue the musicians to play softly so that he could tell the audience about the kingdom and the characters. The musicians listened for another tap as a cue to resume playing full force when the narration was finished. Once again, the *dhalang* sang a song at the end of the main piece.

In the course of the scene, the *dhalang* sang a more intense song to express heightened emotion and cued the musicians to play "Srepeg Nem" when Gathutkaca sent one of his uncles off to call his rebellious prime minister back to court. At the end of the scene, "Srepeg Nem" was played once again to escort the characters as they left the meeting. Gathutkaca used his ability to fly so that he could spy on the meeting between his emissary and the prime minister. To show this, the *dhalang* held the puppet high, casting a shadow near the top of the screen, while holding the *kayon* puppet away from the screen to cast an indistinct cloud-like shadow. He then turned the *kayon* back into a boundary marker as he held it in the middle of the screen to signify the beginning of another scene.

The patterns I have described here recurred several more times in the course of the evening's performance. They represent widely recognized conventions of Javanese theatrical performance, applying first of all to the shadow play, but also (in most respects) to several other types of theater. Before continuing the synopsis of this play, there are important conclusions to draw about the types of music as well as how they function in *wayang* and how they are adapted to the needs of the play.

irama tanggung (irama 1)

```
 +   +   )   +   (   +   )   +   (   +   )   +   (   +   +  (1)
 i   6   5   3   i   5   3   6   3   5   i   6   5   3   2  (1)
 +   +   )   +   (   +   )   +   (   +   )   +   (   +   +  (2)
 5   3   2   1   5   2   1   3   1   2   5   3   2   3   3  (2)
 +   +   )   +   (   +   )   +   (   +   )   +   (   +   +  (3)
 6   5   3   2   6   3   2   5   2   3   6   5   3   5   5  (3)
```

transition to *irama lancar* (*irama 1/2*) played while speeding up

```
 +   +   )   +   (   +   )   +   (   +   )   +   (   +   +  (1)
 i   6   5   3   i   5   3   6   3   5   i   6   5   3   ·  (1)
                                                       +   +
                                                       ·   2
```

irama lancar (*irama 1/2*)

```
 +       +   )   +       (   +       )   +       (   +       )   +
 ·   2   ·   1   ·   2   ·   3   ·   2   ·   3   ·   5   ·   3   ·   2
 +       (   +       )   +       (   +       )   +       (   +       (3)
 ·   3   ·   5   ·   6   ·   5   ·   6   ·   5   ·   3   ·   2   ·   1
 +       )   +       (   +       )   +       (   +       )   +       (1)
 ·   5   ·   3   ·   2   ·   1   ·   5   ·   3   ·   2   ·   3   ·   2
```

irama dadi (*irama 2*) to *irama tanggung* (*irama 1*); go to second line

```
 +           (       +           )       +           (       +           )       +           (       +           )       +       +       +
 i   6   i   6   5   3   5   3   i   6   i   6   5   3   5   3   i   6   i   6   5   3   5   3   2   3   2   3   ·   2   ·   1
```

transition to *irama lancar* (*irama 1/2*) played while speeding up; go to second line

```
 +           (       +           )       +           (       +           )       +       +       +       +
 5   3   2   1   5   3   2   1   5   3   2   1   5   3   2   1   ·   3   ·   2   ·   1   3   ·   2  (2)
```

FIGURE 7.2 "Lancaran Singa Nebah Sléndro," as performed by Hardo Budoyo, 1991 (CD track 34). Note that the slenthem lags by half a beat in irama 1 and 2.

123

WAYANG REPERTOIRE

The music mentioned in this description of a *wayang* represents three substantially different types of composition: *dhalang* songs; short, fast pieces with very short gong cycles; and pieces with relatively long gong cycles played more slowly. Each is suited to a different purpose: The *dhalang*'s songs express emotions and demarcate boundaries in the performance structure, the pieces with short gong cycles are used to accompany action, and the large-scale pieces provide scope for setting the scene when a king or some other important figure holds audience. Each of these categories is used in each of the three acts (or *pathet*) of a *wayang* performance, with certain pieces specific to each *pathet*.

Music for Expressing Emotion: Sulukan.   The *dhalang* has three types of songs, collectively called *sulukan*, with which to express dramatic mood (which is why they are often called mood songs in English writing about *wayang*). They differ in instrumentation and, more subtly, in pacing and other musical characteristics. *Pathetan* have the fullest accompaniment, consisting of *rebab*, *gendèr*, *gambang*, and *suling*. Most vocal phrases consist of a reiterated pitch with little melodic motion. The idiomatic patterns played on each instrument serve to reinforce those *sèlèh*. This chant-like song conveys serenity. *Pathetan* serve to reinforce the mode (*pathet*); certain ones are also used as markers at the boundaries between scenes and acts (CD track 35).

   Sendhon are similar to *pathetan* but they do not normally involve the *rebab*, and their melodies have more pronounced contours (i.e., fewer monotone phrases). "Sendhon Tlutur" (CD track 36) expresses sadness through use of *barang miring*, which features several pitches outside the *sléndro* scale, giving the effect of *pélog* superimposed on *sléndro*. You heard this in the *irama* 2 section of "Ladrang Asmaradana" (CD track 27, 1:59–3:47).

   The third type of song, *ada-ada*, is the most intense and the most frequently performed. It can express anger, tension, and excitement. Accompanied only on *gendèr*, it has the most melodic motion and the greatest intensity due not only to its rapidity but to the *dhalang*'s insistent tapping on the puppet box or the bronze plates of the *kepyak* while singing (CD track 2).

   In addition to the instrumentation mentioned, every *sulukan* also involves occasional strokes on gong, *kenong*, and *kempul*. These sounds serve to reinforce the ends of phrases, timed to add emphasis to the *dhalang*'s final syllable. They are not colotomic in function; there is no shared pulse, so there can be no regular recurrence of gong strokes and hence no colotomic structure.

Unlike the song texts introduced in chapter 4, the *sulukan* texts are not *macapat* written in the eighteenth or nineteenth century but selections from far older works of Javanese poetry, mostly versions of the Mahabharata and Ramayana. Thus the texts are usually relevant to performances of episodes from these epics even though they are not composed for a specific performance. The language is different enough from modern Javanese that many Javanese do not understand every word, but they can still respond to the texts, sensing the overall mood and hearing the past evoked through the same poetry sung in every *wayang*.

One of the most common texts sung to "Pathetan Sléndro Sanga Wantah" (CD track 35). will serve to illustrate the serenity evoked by a *pathetan*:

Sangsaya dalu araras abyor kang lintang kumedhap
tistis sonya tengah wengi,
lumrang gandaning puspita
karengwan ing pudyanira,
sang dwijawara mbrengengeng
lir swaraning madubrangta
manungsung sarining kembang

This translates roughly as follows:

The night becomes lovelier, the stars twinkle. It is cool and still in the middle of the night and the sweet smell of flowers spreads. The murmured chant of the holy men is like bees humming, seeking the flowers' pollen.

Since the beginning of a *wayang*'s second act, Pathet Sanga, occurs around midnight, this text is appropriate to any *wayang* performance. It is even more relevant to the many plays in which the second act begins with the hero at a holy man's hermitage. Similarly, the *pathetan* that initiates the third act, "Pathetan Sléndro Manyura Wantah," begins with the words "mèh rahina," meaning "it is almost dawn" —which it usually is at this point in the show (CD track 37).

By contrast, *ada-ada* texts often concern battle or natural tumult. For instance, as the army is about to march off on its mission in the fourth scene (see above), the *dhalang* usually sings "Ada-ada Budhalan Mataraman" (CD track 2). The standard text for this, linked to the medieval *Serat Bratayudha Kawi-Miring*, describes the huge army of the Pandawas marching off, roaring, in the morning, their uniforms shining like the sun that rises out of the ocean to light the world. Ki Sutino sang this text even though the army in this performance was led by the Kurawas and not by their rivals, the Pandawas. It is the imagery and the symbolic import of the song that matter.

ACTIVITY 7.4   *Study the melodic contour graph of the vocal part to "Pathetan Sléndro Sanga Wantah" (see figure 7.3) while listening to CD track 35. Now use the bottom half of the figure to diagram the contour of "Pathetan Sléndro Manyura Wantah" (CD track 37). The text is a bit longer (a slash indicates a phrase break):*

Mèh rahina semubang ywang haruna kadi netraning /
Angga rapuh sabdaning kukila / O . . . ring kanigara saketer /
O . . . / Kinidungan ing kung / Lir wuwusing pinipanca
O . . . / Papetog ing ayam wana / O . . .

It is almost dawn. The blood-red sun is like an eye in a tired body. The voice of a bird on a sunflower is like the quivering singing of a beloved. Like the sigh of a distressed man is the cackling of the wood-hen.

What similarities do you notice between these two songs? What differentiates them from one another?

The three types of *sulukan* are sung in all three acts, but the specific pieces are different in each *pathet*. The titles of these pieces tell you the type of piece (*pathetan, sendhon,* or *ada-ada*) and the tuning and mode (*sléndro nem, sanga,* or *manyura*) in which it is performed. The word *wantah* in the title "Pathetan Sléndro Sanga Wantah" means "pure" and indicates that this is the basic *pathetan* in that mode. Other *pathetan* in that mode are related to this by abbreviation, extension, or substitution of a phrase or two. Each is a *pathetan*, similar in melodic character and musical texture but distinct in melody, text, and dramatic function. They all differ from any *sendhon* or *ada-ada*.

ACTIVITY 7.5   *Listen to CD tracks 35, 36, and 2. Describe the differences in singing and accompaniment. How do you think these differences help to evoke the contrasting moods of calm, sadness, and tension associated with these three song genres?*

Music for Accompanying Motion: **Gendhing Lampah.**   As important as a *dhalang's* songs are in a performance of *wayang*, they account for a relatively small portion of the music. A far greater portion of the performance soundscape is filled by pieces featuring the louder instruments of the ensemble played in fast, densely packed textures, with ringing gongs that mark very short cycles and rapid drumming that follows the puppets and amplifies their movements. These pieces are sometimes called irregular because the gong phrases vary in length within a single piece and from one composition to the next. In keeping with this irregularity, such pieces have relatively flexible drum parts. They also have a short ending (four to eight beats long) that can be played almost at a moment's notice. Flexibility on many levels makes such pieces suitable to accompany action in theatrical performances since they can readily be adapted to the needs of the moment. Collectively they are sometimes called *gendhing lampah* ("walking pieces").

Just as the *dhalang*'s songs (*sulukan*) are subdivided into three types to express different emotions, three types of *gendhing lampah* convey a sense of motion that ranges from the measured movement of gods and kings to the intensity of a fight to the death. The three types of *gendhing lampah* have distinct names, moods, performance conventions, and theatrical associations. Performers may stray from these conventions— there has been considerable innovation in this area in recent years— but there is a broadly shared sense of the appropriateness of piece types for particular types of action. A glance at figure 7.4 shows that *sampak* is the most intense. It can be played soft or loud, at a moderate to very rapid speed. It is played for tense moments such as mortal combat and magical transformations. The same sorts of colotomic parts characterize a *srepeg*, but the distribution of *kenong* and *kempul* strokes is half as dense. *Srepeg* is the workhorse of the *gendhing lampah* repertoire, played very frequently in theater and dance performances. It is useful for accompanying movement of characters as they travel or enter and exit the stage as we saw in "Brajadenta Balela." It can also be used for battle scenes, though the most intense moments will be accompanied by *sampak*. The most sedate form, the *ayak-ayakan*, has the least dense colotomic structure. Pieces in this form are considered to convey a more regal mood than the *sampak* and *srepeg*. They commonly accompany gods descending from the heavens or a king leaving his palace. They may also accompany the soul of a dead warrior as it rises from the body. As with *sulukan*, the three types of *gendhing lampah* differ in instrumentation: the full gamelan performs *ayak-ayakan*, the *rebab* is not used in *srepeg*, and the rest of the soft elaborating instruments (*gendèr, gambang, siter, suling*) do not participate in *sampak*. The *pesindhèn* sings in *ayak-ayakan* and *srepeg* (except when it is played fast).

Pathetan Sléndro Sanga Wantah

O

2̇ |

i | O ...

6 |

5 | nira

3 |

2 | O ...   O ... karengwan   Sang dwijawara   Lir   Manung-
         ing pudyan-   mbrenge-

1 | sonya tengah wengi lumrang   swaraning   sung sarining
Sangsaya dalu araras abyor Tistis   gandaning puspita   madubrangta   kem-
kang lintang kumedap

6̣ | ngeng

5̣ | bang

Pathetan Sléndro Manyura Wantah

$\dot{3}$

$\dot{2}$

$\dot{1}$

6

5

3   Meh rahina semubang

2

1

.6

.5

.3

FIGURE 7.3 *Contour graph of "Pathetan Sléndro Sanga Wantah" with a grid for graphing "Pathetan Sléndro Manyura Wantah" (see CD tracks 35 and 37 and Activity 7.4).*

Sampak

beat	kethuk	kenong	kempul	gong
	t	N		
•		N	P	
	t	N		
•		N	P	
	t	N		
•		N	P	
	t	N		
•		N	P	G

replaces the 8th or 12th *kempul* stroke depending on the melodic phrase length

Srepeg

beat	kethuk	kenong	kempul	gong
	t	N		
•				
	t	N	P	
•				
	t	N		
•			P	
	t	N		
•				G

replaces the 4th, 8th, or 12th *kempul* stroke depending on the melodic phrase length

Ayak-ayakan

beat	kethuk	kenong	kempul	gong
	t			
•				
	t	N		
•				
	t			
•			P	
	t	N		
•				G

may replace *kempul*

FIGURE 7.4 *Colotomic patterns for gendhing lampah. These patterns are adjusted to fit the melodic phrases of specific pieces. At the end of a phrase a stroke on gong ageng or gong suwukan replaces the kempul as heard on CD tracks 33 and 38.*

Notice the following relationships between the colotomic instruments and the pulse of the *balungan* as you study figure 7.4. In every case, the *kethuk* provides the drive by playing between the beats and pushing toward the following beat. With its dry, relatively "dead" timbre (remember that strokes on the *kethuk* are damped), it cuts through the texture. Listen for this on CD track 38. Note that the high-pitched *kempyang* is not played at all. The *kenong* is played twice as often as *kempul*, so it is lower in the hierarchy of subdivisions of a cycle. Furthermore, *gendhing lampah* are the only colotomic forms in which *kempul* and *kenong* are struck simultaneously. *Gong suwukan* (or occasionally *ageng*) replaces *kempul* at phrase endings, so *kempul* and gong are treated as if they were two parts of one instrument.

All *gendhing lampah* begin with a brief drum pattern (as little as one stroke!), not with the melodic introductions characteristic of longer forms such as *ketawang* and *ladrang*. This is part of their utility as dramatic vehicles: they can start at a moment's notice. They also have short ending melodies, which can be tacked on almost anywhere at a cue from the drummer. Again, this enhances the suitability of such pieces for dramatic action. It is possible to move between any of these forms at a cue from the drummer in order to reflect shifting moods or new actions on the stage or screen. It is easy to move seamlessly from one to another thanks to the many similarities in the flow of their melodies.

ACTIVITY 7.6 *Listen to CD track 38. Note the time code when the musicians go from the fast "Sampak Manyura" to the slower "Ayak-ayakan Manyura." What do you hear that might be cueing the musicians to do this? What changes other than speed?*

The success of such rapid transitions from one piece to another depends partly on the close melodic relationships among the basic *sampak*, *srepeg*, and *ayak-ayakan* in a given *pathet*. As with *sulukan*, there are different *gendhing lampah* in each *pathet*. For instance, the piece "Sampak Manyura" has the same basic colotomic structure as "Sampak Sanga" and "Sampak Nem," but each has a distinctive melody. The same can be said for pieces in *ayak-ayakan* or *srepeg* form in the three *pathet*.

ACTIVITY 7.7 *Try to characterize the melodic relationship between "Srepeg Manyura" and "Sampak Manyura" based on figure*

> 7.5. Can you formulate rules that explain the transformation of the
> "Srepeg" melody into the "Sampak"? Now listen to these pieces in
> succession on CD track 21 starting at 6:39 ("Sampak Manyura"
> starts at 7:33).

The melodies of the basic *srepeg* and *sampak* within a given *pathet* are
so closely related that they can be conceived as two manifestations of
the same piece. Even most of their drum patterns can be shared. (The
relationship to the corresponding *ayak-ayakan* is not quite as close.)
Musicians are aware of these connections and must master transfor-
mational processes that allow them to pass between related pieces at
a moment's notice. In several of the *pathet*, there are other *ayak-ayakan,*
srepeg, and *sampak* forms. The ones given here are considered the basic
ones and are played most frequently.

Music for Setting a Scene: Gendhing. In addition to music for
emotion and motion, the *wayang* requires music for setting a scene.
"Brajadenta Balela" began, like almost every *wayang* performance,
with an audience scene in which a king (in this case the eldest
Kurawa brother, Duryudana) meets with advisors and others in his
throne room. Such scenes tend to be highly formalized, unfolding at
a slow, deliberate pace. As the musicians play, the *dhalang* brings on
the characters one by one, building a tableau. In most performances,
several scenes will be structured in this manner. The fourth scene of
"Brajadenta Balela" is another instance of an audience scene, set in
Gathutkaca's kingdom.

Pieces appropriate for such scenes are chosen from a repertoire of
hundreds of compositions belonging to the category *gendhing*. The
repertoire is divided by tuning system into *pélog* and *sléndro* pieces
and further subdivided by *pathet*; in general each piece belongs to only
one *pathet* and is therefore only appropriate to the act of a *wayang* that
is associated with that *pathet*. Furthermore, in the Solonese *wayang*
tradition—centered in but not limited to the royal courts—specific
gendhing were assigned to particular types of scenes and even to particular characters.

Gendhing are constructed on the basis of long, regular gong cycles,
symmetrically divided into two or four *kenong* phrases. These phrases
may be as short as 8 beats or as long as 64, yielding gong cycles ranging from 16 beats (two phrases of 8 beats) to 256 (four phrases of 64
beats). You already learned about the shortest of these, the *ketawang*

"Sampak Manyura"
2̂ [:2222 3333 1111 1111 2222 6666 3333 2222̂:] suwuk xx22̂

"Srepeg Manyura"
2̂ [:3232 5353 2321 2121 3232 5616̂ 1̇61̇6 5353 6532̂:] suwuk 3232 6532̂

"Ayak-ayakan Manyura"
2̂ .3.2̂ .3.2̂ .5.3̂ .2.1̂

[:2321 2321 3532̂ 3532 5356̂ 5356 5323̂ 5323 6532̂ 6532 3532̂ 3532 5323̂ 5323 2121̂ 2121:]
suwuk 1121̂ 1121 321⑥

FIGURE 7.5 *Basic sampak, srepeg, and ayak-ayakan in pathet sléndro manyura. Only gong ageng and gong suwukan are indicated. Other parts can be inferred from figure 7.4, but note that the ayak-ayakan is exceptional: gong suwukan is played throughout, rather than follow any gong stroke. This is also the case for "Srepeg Manyura" when it is part of the "Talu." The ending phrase (suwuk) of each piece may follow any gong stroke. For "Sampak Manyura" the suwuk is adjusted to match the melodic context, as indicated by xx22, where x represents the last note of the previous phrase.*

133

and *ladrang*. The very longest are seldom (if ever) performed in *wayang* because it would take too long to get the characters on the screen since they can only enter as the *kenong* or gong is struck. The medium and long *gendhing* are differentiated from short-cycle pieces such as *ketawang* and *ladrang*: first, because they have at least two main sections; second, because they have a much sparser colotomic structure. It is customary to delay the *kenong* and gong strokes considerably in such pieces. Not only are the various gong types played less frequently, but *kempul* and *kempyang* are not played in the first section, which is performed in a calm manner in *irama* 2. The second section is often considerably livelier—the *kempyang* is added, the *kethuk* strokes are doubled in number, and the drumming is often more complex. Furthermore, the density may range from *irama* 2 through 3 to 4 (i.e., from medium to greatest expansion, though the greatest expansion is rarely used in *wayang* because it lasts too long).

Unlike *gendhing lampah*, which begin with a cue tapped on the puppet box followed by a specific drum rhythm, *gendhing* begin with a verbal cue. The *dhalang* incorporates the title of the *gendhing* or an oblique reference to that title into the last line of his narration. This is followed by a melodic introduction played on *rebab*, *gendèr*, or *bonang* (depending on the particular piece). The drummer joins in to stabilize the beat and to cue the rest of the musicians to join in. After the piece is well under way, the *dhalang* begins to bring out the characters, one at a time, each appearing on the screen at the end of a phrase. The longer the phrases, the slower the pacing of these entrances is. When he has brought out all of the puppets he intends to use for the scene, the *dhalang* gives another cue, a single tap on the puppet box, strategically timed to a certain point in the gong cycle. The drummer immediately begins to accelerate and the others follow suit, playing louder as they approach the end of the cycle. At the end of the first phrase of the next cycle, the *dhalang* and drummer give further cues to slow the music down to its previous pace (or somewhat slower). Most of the musicians stop playing so that only the soft sounds of the *rebab* and *gendèr* remain with sparse drumming and colotomic instruments to serve as background for narration. When the *dhalang* completes his narration, he gives a further cue, tapping and singing, to tell the musicians to resume playing as a full ensemble. In response, *saron*, *bonang*, and various elaborating instruments are heard again, and the drummer resumes a louder, more complex drumming style. Such changes in orchestration and volume are used at various points in a *wayang* to enable the *dhalang* to narrate over softer musical background, as you can hear on CD track 32.

RETURN TO "BRAJADENTA BALELA"

With these basic components in mind, it is now possible to recount the rest of Ki Sutino's performance of "Brajadenta Balela" in brief. To the sounds of "Srepeg Nem," the rebellious ogre uncle Brajadenta flees from his nephew, King Gathutkaca (see figure 6.4). The *dhalang*'s narrative voice and the appearance of the *kayon* signal a change of scene. The intense "Sampak Nem" is played as Brajadenta enters the forest of death, where ghosts and demons taunt him. He ignores them, awaiting Durga, goddess of the dead (see figure 6.4). "Sampak" changes to "Ayak-ayakan Nem" for her entrance. She makes a pact with Brajadenta, offering him protection in exchange for his soul. She then transforms him to look exactly like his nephew, Gathutkaca, and tells him to go off to the kingdom of Astina to pursue Queen Banowati.

"Pathetan Sléndro Sanga Wantah" (which you heard in Activity 7.4) and a sentence or two of narration mark the beginning of the second *pathet*. With a verbal cue, the *dhalang* requests a *gendhing*. In accordance with the *gendhing*'s phrase structure, he brings out Arjuna with his three servants, Semar and his two sons, Garèng and Petruk (see figure 6.5). When they are onstage, the *dhalang* cues the gamelan to accelerate and then drop back to soft accompaniment so that he can tell the audience that Arjuna has just left the hermitage of Abiyasa (grandfather of the Pandawas and their cousins, the Kurawas). After the narration, a cue brings the gamelan back at full volume with lively drumming as the musicians proceed to the *inggah* section. Semar and his sons dance to the music.

Semar is a god, punished for his arrogance by being sent to earth to serve men. He is wise and crude, capable of being both serious and funny. His sons are always squabbling, rarely serious, often hilarious. They make their appearance in the second *pathet* of every *wayang*, often with a third son, Bagong. They serve Arjuna or some other knight, but they also represent Javanese commoners, speaking everyday low Javanese rather than the high theatrical language used by many of the other characters. Through them, the *dhalang* interacts with the *pesindhèn*, requesting songs purely for entertainment rather than to set a scene, accompany a battle, or move the drama onward in some way. This interlude in the action can last an hour or more. It is often the time that the host sponsoring the *wayang* will have dinner served to the guests. In the abbreviated performance in a Berkeley church, there was no food and only one song rather than the customary string of popular songs that show off the voices of several singers.

Arjuna walks off (followed by his servants) and meets Cakil, a forest demon who always appears at this juncture. "Srepegan Sanga" provides the accompaniment for this confrontation. Cakil skitters across the screen, taunting Arjuna, who barely acknowledges his presence (see figure 6.5). The *dhalang* displays his dexterity by having Cakil bounce a dagger along his arm. The musicians shift to the more intense "Sampak Sanga" when Cakil is stabbed with his own dagger—Arjuna is so powerful that he barely needs to move to kill the demon. An ogre enters and the music is brought to a halt. The *dhalang* sings an *ada-ada* to express the tension of this new confrontation and then cues "Sampak Sanga" for the ensuing battle in which Arjuna overcomes this ogre and another. The statelier "Ayak-ayakan Sanga" accompanies the victorious Arjuna as he continues on his way.

A new scene takes place back in Astina, site of the opening of this performance. The *dhalang* cues a *ladrang* as background to bringing out Queen Banowati and Brajadenta, disguised as his nephew, Gathutkaca. After the piece ends, Brajadenta makes advances, which Banowati repulses; he leaves and "Srepegan Sanga" is played to bring on the Prime Minister of Astina. Banowati tells him what has happened. They both think that it is the real Gathutkaca who has insulted the queen. "Srepegan Sanga" is played again as the Kurawa brothers fight the false Gathutkaca but fail because he is invincible. "Srepegan Sanga" then accompanies the Prime Minister as he sets off to tell King Duryudana (see figure 6.6). A final intense "Sampak Sanga" ends the act.

"Pathetan Manyura Wantah" (CD track 37) marks the beginning of the third and final *pathet*. Again the *dhalang* cues a *gendhing* so that he can set the scene. This time it takes place in the throne room of King Yudhistira, eldest of the Pandawas. He meets with his brothers (except Arjuna who is traveling). Again there is a soft section for narration. Duryudana, king of the Kurawas, enters. The piece is followed by a shorter version of "Pathetan Sléndro Manyura Wantah" to mark the end of the *gendhing*. The characters begin to speak but are soon interrupted by "Ayak-ayakan Manyura" for the arrival of a messenger to tell Bima that his son Gathutkaca is ill. No sooner has this been recounted than the far more urgent "Sampak Manyura" is played for the entrance of the Prime Minister of Astina. He has come to tell Duryudana (his king) of the affront to Queen Banowati, supposedly caused by Gathutkaca. The reaction is outrage; none is angrier than Gathutkaca's father, Bima (see figure 6.4). A quick rhythmic cue, tapped on the puppet box, starts "Sampak Manyura" to accompany the departure of all the characters. Bima is shown racing over mountains until he reaches Gathutkaca's kingdom and confronts him. His son pleads innocence, so they depart for Astina to see who has impersonated Gathutkaca there. Several more performances of "Sampak Manyura" accompany their travel and the battle between the real and false Gathutkacas. For the climactic battle, the musicians switch from the usual "Sampak Manyura" to a piece with *sampak* colotomic structure but a shorter melody (1111 6666 3333 2222) that heightens the intensity. A mighty blow from Gathutkaca returns Brajadenta to his true form. The fight continues until Gathutkaca kills Brajadenta. As his soul leaves his body, it meets the goddess of the dead, Durga, whose protection was not as strong as Gathutkaca. The drummer cues the musicians to switch to "Ayak-ayakan Manyura," the type of *gendhing lampah* appropriate to the stately motion of gods.

Bima raises his arms. This is a visual cue to switch to "Ladrang Sigra Mangsah" to the sounds of which Bima does a victory dance. Once again he raises his arm as a cue to switch to the concluding piece, "Ayak-ayakan Pamungkas." This begins like a normal "Ayak-ayakan Manyura" but slows down to an expanded *irama* to accommodate a choral song before reverting to regular "Ayak-ayakan." During this time the *dhalang* brings on the Pandawas and their allies to form a final tableau around the *kayon*, which is planted in the center of the screen.

ACTIVITY 7.8 *Make a chart of the play I have described, with the dramatic action in one column and the corresponding music to its right in a second column so that you can review the overall progression of events and how music was used at different points. Now take the plot of a story you know (such as a fairy tale or a play by Shakespeare) and write up a synopsis indicating the Javanese music you think appropriate for each scene or moments within a scene.*

How did this performance compare to a typical *wayang* in Java? It included many of the common elements of a full-length *wayang* performance, and it was condensed in ways that are common in Java when a short performance is needed. Toward the end of the play, Ki Sutino was clearly rushing in order to fit it into two and a half hours, but in the beginning his pacing was relatively leisurely. Once he reached Washington for his residency at the Smithsonian, he had to adapt further to present one-hour shows three times a day. These differed from shows in Java most significantly due to the linguistic and cultural barriers to communication with his American audience. The *dhalang* spoke no English and did not try to remake the show in a manner that would appeal to Americans other than abbreviating it. For their part, most of the audience did not understand Javanese and lacked any knowledge of the conventions and content of this theatrical tradition. Thus they did not have the expectations that Ki Sutino was used to fulfilling. Because puppet shows in the United States usually are aimed at children, some people brought little children who quickly got bored by the extended music, dialogue, and narration in a foreign language. Had they stayed to the end, they would likely have been entertained by all the action. The lack of direct intelligibility did not deter everyone; some spectators stayed till the end and clamored for more.

ACTIVITY 7.9 *Attend an "exotic" performance from a culture completely foreign to you or watch one on TV. Try to recall any explanations that you received before or during the performance. How did they affect your experience? Do you think that performers or those who present them have a responsibility to explain, interpret, or contextualize, or do you feel that such mediation detracts from the directness of artistic expression? In group discussion or a paper, debate the various sides of the challenges of cross-cultural communication.*

One of the barriers to cross-cultural acceptance is a *wayang's* dramatic pace. The beginning is slow—half an hour or more of music can precede the show—and the end consists again of music during which the audience usually leaves. Almost everything, from the entire performance down to individual scenes, is framed or "book-ended" by opening and closing music. Such framing is particularly evident in the more formal audience scenes, which begin with a fairly lengthy *gendhing*, followed by a song and a formal exchange of greetings before the story comes to the fore. The end of such a scene often consists of a leave-taking only slightly shorter and less formalized than its beginning. The entire show is framed by the *talu* at the beginning and an *ayak-ayakan* at the end. As the opening, the *talu* has symbolic importance on at least two levels: its constituent pieces represent stages in human life from birth to death, and they provide a sort of catalog of the types of music that will be used in the performance (including both scene-setting pieces and the three types of "walking pieces"). Only the *dhalang's* songs are absent from this overture, and with good reason. He may wait to mount the stage until the *talu* is played, or he may choose to play with the gamelan.

FLEXIBILITY AND APPROPRIATENESS

The high degree of spontaneity in *wayang*, with many of the details decided only at the moment of performance, means that the music must often be suited to the needs of the action, but there are also moments when the action is made to fit the music. Thus there is a degree of reciprocity between music and drama. The balance between the two shifts, depending on the situation. When the *dhalang* is setting a scene to the accompaniment of a *gendhing*, he is bound by the structure of that *gendhing*. On the other hand, when he enacts a battle, the music is shaped to suit his needs, starting and stopping with very little warning. Even so, he remains cognizant of the music's structure and coordinates most of the decisive moves with gong strokes. All of this requires not only great flexibility of the musicians but also means of communication that ensure tight coordination.

The success of a *wayang* performance depends on the interaction between *dhalang* and musicians. As you have seen in the description of the performance of "Brajadenta Balela," the *dhalang* cues the musicians not only to begin and end pieces but to change volume and speed or switch from one piece to another. This highly conventionalized cueing includes tapping rhythms on the puppet box or on the overlapping metal plates hanging on the box, singing, speaking, or putting the puppets in particular positions. The responses must be precisely timed—if each musician were to respond independently, chaos might result. The drummer mediates most of the cues; however, other performers may take the lead at times, primarily when performing the melodic introductions to longer pieces. Interaction between the musicians and the *dhalang* often extends beyond music: the *dhalang* will make inside jokes about the musicians that only they may understand, and they may laugh in response or call out to egg him on.

The drummer is key not only to managing most of the communication between the *dhalang* and the musicians but to animating the puppets' movements with his drumming, often with specific sequences that the *dhalang* and the drummer have worked out. This is one of the reasons a *dhalang* prefers to work regularly with a particular drummer. For example, in addition to relaying the *dhalang*'s cues, he supplies sound effects that augment puppets' blows in a fight. He plays standard drum patterns, appropriate to the type of piece (*ladrang* or *sampak*, for instance), but once the music is under way, he often abandons those patterns in order to follow the puppets' movements. Since many of the accents that he plays fall between the beats, the other musicians must learn to filter them out, maintaining a steady beat and responding only to those drum strokes which constitute cues. The *dhalang*, too, supplies sound effects with his mallet. One of the more challenging aspects of accompanying a *wayang* is to distinguish between sound effects and cues.

The question of appropriateness underlies all such interpretative decisions. Radical departures from what has been considered appropriate are possible, of course, but they strain the conventions of interaction that ensure a smooth performance. The use of music appropriate to a given scene or character is hardly questioned, and a drummer's ability to produce patterns appropriate to a given character's style of movement is highly valued. This is not where Javanese performers have sought to innovate.

CONVENTIONS AND INNOVATIONS

Javanese *wayang* performances rely heavily on conventions. Even avant-garde performances—and there have been many in Indonesia since the 1980s—have some relation to conventions as they flout earlier ones and contribute to the emergence of new ones (particularly if these performances are repeated, varied, or emulated by others). The importance of these conventions differs depending on one's position within the performance arena: for the *dhalang*, they are the tools to creating or re-creating a story; for the musicians, they are the means for interpreting the *dhalang*'s desires in concerted performance; for the spectators, they provide the framework for understanding what the performers present.

A *dhalang* structures a performance in relation to conventions, usually following them, sometimes altering them, or even expressly defying them. Musicians rely on their knowledge of *wayang* conventions to interpret the *dhalang*'s cues in order to know when to play, what to play, and how to play it. Knowledge of conventions allows people to enter in the middle of a show and not be too disoriented or leave before the end and be able to imagine how the end might be. It enables those who hear radio broadcasts and cassettes to imagine what they are missing. Seeing the shadow side is not always possible; even when it is, the majority of the audience is often to be found on the lighted side of the screen, watching the *dhalang* at work and sitting close to the musicians. When I returned to Solo after the *wayang* described in chapter 6, the man next to me on the bus explained to me that he chooses to sit in a place where he cannot see the screen because he prefers to respond to the images evoked by the *dhalang*'s words. This only works because he has seen many performances and has internalized the characters and the conventions.

Of course, a completely conventional performance might not be exciting or artistically rewarding, and it might not add to a *dhalang*'s professional reputation, bringing him additional invitations to perform—but then again, it might. This brings up a fundamental difference between *wayang* and movies or the various other theatrical performances common in the Uinted States, for instance. While *wayang* is enjoyed as entertainment, it almost always serves a ritual purpose as well; to satisfy ritual requirements, it need not break new artistic ground.

Javanese performers have experimented with many innovations in *wayang* in recent years. They have compressed shows to as little as 45 minutes, involved more than one *dhalang*, created new puppets, invented new stories and composed new music. Radically abbreviated shows have required new approaches to the use of music. While they can be highly unconventional in themselves, they often assume deep knowledge of *wayang* conventions on the part of performers and audiences.

In full-length performances, traditional musical repertoire has been retained but is often augmented by new pieces or altered here and there (but not everywhere) by new arrangements. Even the most commonly played pieces are not immune to change. The *saron* parts for *sampak* and *srepeg* seem to undergo continual variation, and the drumming for such pieces changes, too.

Perhaps more striking is the emergence of arrangers/composers who actually mold the repertoire for an entire show. B. Subono, whom you heard singing *pathetan* on CD tracks 35 and 37, is a prominent example. A *dhalang* in his own right, Subono has composed new pieces and arranged existing ones for use in *wayang* performances by others, including Midiyanto. These arrangements require considerable rehearsal, in stark contrast to traditional *wayang* in which the conventions have been known widely enough and in sufficient depth to allow the musicians and *dhalang* to put on a performance without rehearsal. The arrangements are also technically difficult, enabled by the virtuosity fostered in the hothouse atmosphere of the performing arts academy in Solo where Subono is a member of the faculty.

Musical innovation has extended to include of other styles of music and other instruments alongside the usual gamelan. Bass and snare drums have been borrowed from Western popular music and marching bands to augment the Javanese *kendhang* for accents in battle scenes. Some *dhalangs* have incorporated the catchy virtuosic dance drumming of *jaipongan* (a style of popular music that emerged in West Java in the early 1980s) in their performances, going so far as to include a second drummer who specializes in that style and its particular drums and playing techniques.

What has motivated these innovations? Some doubtless resulted from particular individuals' desire for experimentation and personal expression. Economic pressures to compete in the marketplace have also driven performers to seek new ways to entertain and to make a mark. This was particularly the case as Indonesia began to emerge from the grip of the authoritarian regime of Suharto in the late 1990s. Audience members became more assertive in their demands, as Santosa found during research for his (University of California) dissertation on village *wayang* (2001). *Dhalangs* tried gimmicks such as employing dancers or comedians to perform in select portions of the show alongside the screen.

The biggest pressure may have been the arrival of an alternative form of live entertainment, the *campursari* mentioned in chapter 1. It was contemporary and emblematic of Indonesian engagement with international trends and a world that had opened up to MTV (a special channel covers Southeast Asia). It had catchy songs, with young female and male singers crooning in a popular song style, and it was cheap. A group of musicians performing *campursari* cost a fraction of a *wayang* performance. When a major financial crisis arose in Southeast Asia in 1997, Indonesia was hit very hard. Suddenly many people who needed to celebrate ritual occasions such as weddings, circumcisions, and anniversaries of other important occurrences could not afford to hire a *dhalang* and gamelan or pay and entertain guests for a full night. A small *campursari* performance saved money in many ways and also offered up-to-date entertainment. To compete, some *dhalangs* incorpo- rated *campursari* in their *wayang* performances. CD track 3 was recorded at a *wayang* performance at Midiyanto's house in Eromoko in 2000. At the time, he was inviting a series of *dhalangs* to perform at his house every 35 days to mark the birth of his eldest son, continuing the tradition of ritual demarcation of a calendrical coincidence (discussed in chapter 1). But he and his invited *dhalang* were also bending to current fashion and providing local youth who had formed a *campursari* group an opportunity to perform. They did this in the middle of the *wayang* night, a time that has long been marked for entertainment, for music that does not advance the plot at all, often in response to audience requests for specific songs (accompanied by gifts of money or cigarettes).

Institutional forces have also affected innovation in *wayang*. Faculty and students at performing arts schools have been encouraged to innovate as part of their program of study. Such performances are usually scripted for several reasons. Extreme abbreviation requires tight coordination—there simply is no margin for error—and use of multiple *dhalangs* (either to provide a variety of voices or to increase the possibilities for puppet manipulation) also changes the interaction among performers. The involvement of several *dhalangs* (as many as 10) brings varied voices and enables speech to overlay song. Performers have experimented with technical means of various sorts, ranging from using new puppet designs and complex lighting (e.g., colored lights) to modifying the screen (e.g., extremely large screens, multiple screens, and painting on the screen).

The aims of the state are served by large-scale productions mounted by faculty and students at the state-run arts schools. The use in some performances of Indonesian language rather than Javanese realizes the national motto of unity in diversity by creating a performance that is more accessible to the majority of Indonesians who are not Javanese. Perhaps the most radical change in such academic experiments, more enduring than any particular innovation, is the conception of the *wayang* performance as a work of art.

CHAPTER 8

Java and Beyond

PAK COKRO

The remarkable career of Kangjeng Pangéran Harya Natapraja, known familiarly to his many students around the world as Pak Cokro, highlights many of the important changes that have taken place in Javanese performing arts over the past century (see figure 8.1). Born in 1909 at the princely court of the Paku Alam in Yogyakarta, he was the natural son of Prince Paku Alam VII himself but was raised as the son of the leader of the court orchestra. Like others associated with Javanese courts, he underwent name changes as he rose in station; he was named Cokrowasito as a young man, then became Wasitodipuro, and later changed to Wasitodiningrat. The latter two names were preceded by the honorific title Kangjeng Radèn Tumenggung, which placed him very high in the traditional hierarchy of social status. In his nineties, he was finally recognized as the son of the late Paku Alam VII and half-brother of Prince Paku Alam VIII. This entailed another change of name and rank as he became a prince: Kangjeng Pangéran Harya Natapraja.

Pak Cokro counts among his ancestors not only royalty and gamelan musicians but dancers and singers of *kakawin*, an old genre of poetry that passed out of oral tradition when he was still a child. He began to study gamelan at the age of five and also became an accomplished dancer. Attaining competence in both these related arts is not unusual. The interconnectedness of Javanese arts encourages such an education, and artists with multiple competencies strengthen such connections.

Although he grew up in Yogyakarta, Pak Cokro learned Solonese gamelan traditions, too. The Prince Paku Alam had married a princess from the Surakarta *kraton*, so the two courts maintained artistic ties. Pak Cokro was sent with a few court musicians to learn the music for dances that were the particular property of the *kraton*. In 1931 (around the time the recording of "Ladrang Sri Katon" excerpted in CD track 5 was made at the *kraton*), he spent a month at the house of the head of the *kraton* musicians. Some of the Solonese musicians also came to the Paku

FIGURE 8.1 *Pak Cokro (K. P. H. Natapraja) and author in the mid 1980s.*
(Photo by Lisa Gold.)

Alaman palace in Yogyakarta. This intensive exposure to Solonese court musicians was a formative experience for Pak Cokro, who still mentioned their names in hushed awe when he told me about them nearly 60 years later. Diplomacy through marriage was responsible for similar artistic connections between the Yogyakarta *kraton* and the Mangkunagaran in Surakarta. At the same time, each court jealously guarded certain performance traditions such as the dances that Pak Cokro learned. Rather than a legal concept of copyright, there was a feudal sense of royal power that held sway prior to Indonesian independence, despite the lack of any real political power under Dutch colonial rule.

Prior to his trip to Solo, Pak Cokro had already sought to increase his understanding of *rebab* technique. Sitting in his house in a California suburb, he told me about visiting the leading musicians in Yogya in the 1920s and asking them, "Do you have any theory about *rebaban* [playing the *rebab*]? Do you have any *culikan* [a short formula for testing the tuning and the mode]? Do you have any technique about the bowing?" Pak Cokro said that he never received clear answers and so developed his own style. This independence and relative lack of guidance are not unusual among Javanese musicians, though Pak Cokro may have been more probing than most in questioning other musicians.

Although certain steps were taken by the courts to institute formal training in the arts in the 1920s, it was only after Indonesian independence that strong institutional frameworks for learning dance, gamelan, and *wayang* arose. Pak Cokro was active in these efforts. He trained many singers at his own school for *pesindhèn* and was also one of the first teachers at the high school conservatory, Konservatori Karawitan, established by the government in Solo in the 1950s. He even served on the selection committee for teachers, testing the musical knowledge of former court musicians who applied for teaching positions. For the last 20 years of his active professional career, Pak Cokro taught in the United States, primarily in California. As part of his teaching, he wrote out notation for hundreds of pieces for his students. His collection of vocal notation can be downloaded at the American Gamelan Institute's website (see Resources).

Pak Cokro took on leadership positions very early. During the Dutch colonial period, at the age of 25, he became music director at a Yogyakarta radio station. He continued when the station came under government control in newly independent Indonesia in 1945, holding the post for almost 40 years. This gave him great influence in musical life. Broadcasts and recordings under his direction contributed to the spread of Solonese compositions and gamelan performance style in an area that had had a distinctive Yogyanese repertoire and style. Pak Cokro also took over direction of the Paku Alaman palace orchestra when his father died.

Pak Cokro also became widely known through his compositions at a time when very few Javanese composers were well known. He rivaled Nartosabdho in influence as a composer (CD track 29; see Becker 1980 for a comparison of the two). These compositions included catchy songs, sometimes with messages that served government needs such as encouraging communal collaboration or educating the public about something as mundane as traffic safety. But his compositional output included far more ambitious efforts. Together with Pak Marto (whom you met in earlier chapters), he composed music for a new form of dance drama. Developed for tourists in the early 1960s, *sendratari* portrayed the Ramayana without dialogue, utilizing hundreds of dancers performing under a full moon at a performance site outside Yogyakarta that exploited the ancient Prambanan temple (see chapter 1) as a spectacular backdrop. In other works Pak Cokro experimented with various musical innovations such as adapting so-called Latin dance rhythms to Javanese *kendhang* and composing for two- or three-part chorus with gamelan. He also composed large-scale musical works that were not subservient to dance, including an hour-long composition that represented a millennium of Javanese history. A good cross-section of his shorter compositions can be heard on *The Music of K.R.T.Wasitodiningrat* (see Resources).

With his numerous international experiences and connections, Pak Cokro is a particularly appropriate figure for a book in a series on global music. He started early in this arena, too, helping his father provide gamelan notation to Walter Spies, a German artist and musician employed at the Yogyakarta *kraton* in the mid-1920s. Spies arranged these gamelan pieces so that Dutch colonials could play them on piano at a time when social barriers probably precluded playing "native" instruments. From the 1950s on, Pak Cokro began to travel on cultural missions to many locations, including Eastern Europe and the 1964 World's Fair in New York. Also in the 1950s, in Yogyakarta, he taught Mantle Hood, who was the first American ethnomusicologist to study Javanese music in depth. Hood was responsible for bringing the first gamelan to UCLA to start instruction in Javanese music and promoting the idea of bi-musicality as a valuable form of education. He was aided by Hardja Susilo, the first Javanese to teach gamelan and study ethnomusicology in the United States (see figure 8.2). Hood's student Robert Brown also formed a close connection with Pak Cokro. Together, they arranged the purchase of Gamelan Kyai Udan Mas for use at the Center for World Music, beginning Pak Cokro's long association with this seminal institution for the teaching of non-Western music, dance, and theater in the United States. Since 1975 the instruments have been at UC Berkeley (figures 2.4 and 3.5; CD tracks 2, 11, 12, 14, 20, 22, 30, 32–34).

Pak Cokro's engagement with non-Javanese included teaching hundreds (perhaps thousands) of students, some of whom have had prominent careers in composition, ethnomusicology, and other arts-related positions. In Berkeley he taught aspects of Javanese music to American composer Lou Harrison, who commissioned Pak Cokro to compose "Gendhing Purnomo Sidhi," featuring a *balungan* especially suited to the extended range of the aluminum *saron* that Harrison and his partner, Bill Colvig, had built. Harrison also honored Pak Cokro by dedicating a composition to him and having a star named for him. This was not the only connection to outer space: A recording of "Ketawang Puspawarna" performed under Pak Cokro's direction (from *Javanese Court Gamelan*, volume 1; see Resources) was one of the few pieces of world music to be sent into space on the *Voyager* spacecraft in 1977 to represent human culture to the universe.

FIGURE 8.2 *Hardja Susilo (left) and Midiyanto (right) have taught and performed Javanese gamelan, dance, and* wayang *outside of Indonesia since the 1950s and 1980s, respectively.* (Photo by Ted Solis.)

INTERCONNECTEDNESS: THEATER, DANCE, AND MUSIC

Pak Cokro's career emphasizes the interconnectedness of the arts, particularly music and dance. The new genre of dance drama that Pak Cokro helped to create in the 1960s was dubbed *sendratari*, combining the words *seni* (art), *drama*, and *tari* (dance). It became a successful form of artistic expression for the arts academies where choreographers and dancers have put together numerous productions over the past few decades, usually taking some episode from Javanese history, legend, or myth as a subject. This type of performance works well in polyglot, multicultural Indonesia because there is no dialogue—linguistic barriers are erased, and it is also more accessible to tourists. It has been adapted in Bali (see Gold 2005: 142).

In the United States Pak Cokro promoted the interconnectedness of the arts, producing dance dramas and incorporating dances into concert programs with the help of his daughter, dancer Nanik Wenten, and his son-in-law, Nyoman Wenten (who wrote a dissertation on Pak Cokro). He taught us about *wayang kulit* and he also had occasion to drum for *wayang* performances, something he would not have done in Java because he was not a specialist in *wayang* drumming. Like other expert Javanese musicians, he can play all the instruments in the gamelan but would rarely have occasion to do so because of his status as director of the orchestra.

Wayang kulit is, in some ways, the crowning glory of Javanese culture, a multimedia extravaganza that can (and often does) draw on every aspect of life. It is thus a manifestation of the interconnectedness of the elements of this culture, suspended in a web of connections to other performing arts. Theater with human actors has taken various forms over the course of Javanese history: some highly scripted and other improvisatory, some performed only by men or only by women, some with masks. That several of these forms have the word *wayang* (shadow) in their name points to the centrality of the shadow play. *Wayang wong*, a popular form of theater performed by actor-dancers with gamelan, emerged at the beginning of the twentieth century and borrowed heavily from *wayang kulit*, including plots and plot structure, iconography of costumes, voices, musical accompaniment, and much more. But *wayang wong* also influenced shadow play performances, leading to the use of a standard large gamelan in both *sléndro* and *pélog* rather than the small *sléndro* gamelan (lacking *bonang* and most of the *saron* "family") that had been customary for *wayang kulit*. The web of connections extends to the many dance choreographies that derive from theatrical genres such as *wayang wong*. Such dance "fragments" are common entertainment at wedding receptions and are also popular at arts schools.

The same ideas about character types that underpin *wayang kulit* are central to dance. Male roles range from highly refined to strong to coarse. It is common to have the most refined male roles danced by women. For instance, the brief excerpts of *lancaran* and *gangsaran* you heard on

CD track 20 come from the accompaniment to "Klana Badra," a dance piece for three performers: a man portraying a coarse, impassioned king in strong male style; a woman dancing in female style to represent the object of the king's desire; and another woman dancing in refined male style, portraying the refined knight who kills the king to defend his love. Drumming style and musical repertoire vary throughout "Klana Badra" according to what is appropriate to the characters on the stage. The powerful *gangsaran* with its loud drumming is particularly appropriate for the king, while a *ketawang* played with softer, more restrained drumming is appropriate when the lovers come on the stage.

Drumming both connects and distinguishes the various performing arts. Dance drumming is inherently different from *wayang* drumming, which differs in turn from *klenèngan* drumming. Drummers usually specialize in one type or another due to these differences, which include the patterns, tempos, types of strokes; even the drum itself may differ. Yet there is substantial borrowing from one genre to another. Thus the *ciblon* patterns that you heard in "Ladrang Asmaradana" (CD track 27) originated in dance drumming but are now ubiquitous in *klenèngan*. They can even be heard in *wayang*. Likewise, the special drumming patterns of *wayang* drumming may be borrowed for *klenèngan* to liven things up. Javanese musicians are keenly aware of such connections and are constantly creating new ones, leading to a thickly entangled set of performance conventions.

Repertoire, too, is shared across performance genres. The same piece may be played for dance, *wayang*, and *klenèngan*. For instance, "Ketawang Subakastawa" (CD track 10) is frequently heard in all three but is treated somewhat differently in each. It is played with standard *ketawang* drum patterns as accompaniment to a refined dance that beginning dancers learn. In *klenèngan*, the same drumming is used, but rather than standing alone, the piece is often linked to the end of a longer two-part *gendhing*, as a contrast to the livelier texture of the *gendhing*'s second section. In performances of *wayang kulit*, "Subakastawa" is played near the beginning of the second *pathet* (act) for the entrance of a knight and his *punakawan* (servant companions). As each character enters, the drumming changes to accompany its characteristic movement style. Often this leads directly into "Ayak-ayakan Sanga," a sequence that can be borrowed in turn for *klenèngan*.

Wayang and *klenèngan* share the large-scale performance structure of three *pathet*. In both cases, the music follows a progression in *sléndro* from *pathet nem* through *sanga* to *manyura*. The parallel progression in *pélog* moves from *pathet lima* through *nem* to *barang*. Musicians exploit these parallel progressions in both *klenèngan* and *wayang* to alternate *sléndro* and *pélog* pieces. These modes affect the way musicians perform elaborating parts; they also divide the repertoire into categories of pieces that are available in each portion of a performance. In other words, the *pathet* system is both a set of categories of musical pieces and a set of ways of performing those pieces appropriately. When he taught me to play *rebab*, Pak Cokro outlined these matters and selected pieces for me to learn so that I would have a well-rounded sense of the possibilities of each *pathet*. Such considerations inform the arts academy curricula, too.

EDUCATIONAL INSTITUTIONS

Pak Cokro had had to seek out knowledge on his own, but as a fully formed musician he became part of the pioneering generation that formalized education in the arts. After World War II and the struggle for independence against the Dutch, the new republic was far more egalitarian in outlook than the feudal ordering of traditional Javanese society. New centers of musical transmission displaced the newly impoverished royal courts as the Indonesian government founded radio stations with full-time musicians, followed by performing arts high schools (conservatories) and colleges (academies) in the 1950s and 1960s. Like Pak Cokro, most of the first teachers at these schools had been court musicians or aristocrats with training in the arts. They codified and formalized the transmission of knowledge relating to music, dance, and theater, a process that had started in court-sponsored schools a few decades earlier but was further systematized, with a broader curriculum no longer bound to one particular palace's traditions.

The schools teach performance practice and repertoire from the courts and the villages. Faculty and students have conducted research on local traditions in villages throughout Central Java and even farther afield. They have also gone to teach in these villages, spreading the practices developed in the arts schools and thus undermining the very diversity that they had documented. This is just one of the delicate issues that have arisen with the institutionalization of arts education. As researchers and teachers write down and publish knowledge that used to be orally transmitted and subject to continual variation, there arises the question whether one should correct "mistakes" that are common practice. For instance, the texts of *sulukan* such as "Pathetan Sanga Wantah," taken from old Javanese versions of the Hindu epics (see chapter 7), exist in numerous variants due to generations of oral transmission. A teacher at the academy decided to locate the corresponding texts in written versions of the epics. The academy published these texts and they became the standard. For many, the written text has higher authority than oral tradition, yet B. Subono, a *dhalang* and teacher who studied at the academy and was taught the "correct" literary versions of the *sulukan* texts there, told me that he could not unlearn everything he had received in oral tradition in his family even though he knew intellectually that he was "mistaken" (CD tracks 35 and 37).

REGIONALISM AND THE DOMINANCE OF SOLONESE STYLE

Central Javanese performing arts have developed over a long span of time and a relatively large territory, engendering numerous localized differences that matter to performers and their audiences. The distinction between the two court cities of Surakarta and Yogyakarta was jealously maintained for over two centuries, so it was no small matter when Pak Cokro used his position at the Yogyakarta radio station to play Surakarta (i.e., Solonese) performance style. His contemporary, Nartosabdho, was famed for introducing the playing style typical of the coastal city of Semarang to the general mix of elements that musicians were creating in the second half of the twentieth century. Although Nartosabdho has been dead for over 20 years, musicians continue to emulate his drumming and perform his compositions, particularly noteworthy for their new approach to vocal parts (recall his reworking of "Ketawang Subakastawa" on CD track 29). Other regional styles, such as the *bonang* playing techniques of Banyumas to the west, have enjoyed some popularity, too (see Sutton 1991). In the late 1990s, a style of playing associated with Sragèn, a town just east of Solo, became especially popular at celebrations, and I heard many musicians complain that audiences were becoming increasingly threatening if the musicians did not give them the Sragèn style they demanded. All these regional styles have been less dominant than the Solonese style that has been favored by the schools, the recording industry, and the radio stations since their inception.

The ascension of Sragèn style at the end of the twentieth century is emblematic of a larger shift away from the refined—some would say stagnant—styles of Solo and Yogya, the royal cities where aristocrats once supported the arts lavishly. The courts cultivated music, dance, and theater not only for entertainment and ritual but also as a central part of a noble's education. They saw the arts as essential to refinement, to the maintenance of Javaneseness. At the same time, village music, dance, and especially *wayang* continued to flourish as a means of communal celebration.

The contrast between village and court is considerable and has been fundamental to discourse about the arts in Central Java (see chapter 5). The prevalent image is a contrast between roughness and refinement, yet much is shared because village and court have a long symbiotic relationship. The courts drew dancers, *dhalangs*, and musicians from the villages and adapted some of their practices. Some of these village artists, in turn, brought court compositions, choreographies, and practices back to their homes. Court musicians, city dwellers, and villagers alike have found gamelan music essential to meditation, self-knowledge, and self-control, relating it to Javanese mysticism and finding expression of inner and outer worlds in this music.

JAVA AND THE REST OF INDONESIA

The arts schools have brought together not only different regional traditions within Central Java but performance practices from other parts of Indonesia. Students encounter a far greater variety of music, dance, and theater than they are likely to learn elsewhere. This includes traditions from West and East Java, Bali, and Sumatra, usually taught by performers from those other parts of Indonesia who have come to teach and study in Central Java.

The variety has inspired some combination and adaptation of ideas and practices from different traditions. Balinese music has had a particularly strong influence on composition, notable, for instance, in the use of very fast tempo, more extensive interlocking, and sudden shifts of mood, tempo, and volume that became commonplace in early-twentieth-century Bali through *kebyar* style (Gold 2005) but gained currency far more recently in Central Java. Such cross-influences serve to promote performances that go beyond Javanese ethnic particularity to create a national Indonesian art, a realization of the national motto *bhinneka tunggal eka*, which means unity in diversity.

JAVA AND THE WORLD

Over the past three decades, Javanese music, dance, and theater have circulated ever more widely, reaching many parts of the world (especially North America, East Asia, Europe, and Australia) through touring performers, artists in residence, recordings, and publications. In reciprocal motion, people from all of those places have traveled to Indonesia to deepen their experience of Javanese expressive culture through study and performance. No matter how wonderful their teachers abroad have been, they gain immeasurably from observing and participating in Javanese music performed in its usual social contexts. Numerous ensembles devoted to Javanese gamelan have emerged outside of Indonesia over the past three decades. Some have focused on staying within Javanese traditions, while others have devoted their efforts to creating new music that may be only remotely related to traditional Javanese gamelan practices. The instruments on which these groups play also vary greatly. Composer Lou Harrison was one of the instigators of building new instruments inspired by Javanese instruments but differing from them in numerous ways, including material (e.g., aluminum plates substitute for gongs), tuning (*sléndro* and *pélog* adapted to just intonation), and range (e.g., *saron* with a range of two octaves rather than one).

ACTIVITY 8.1 *Scan the directory of gamelan groups on the American Gamelan Institute website (see Resources). Many listings are out-of-date, but the list still offers a snapshot of the spread and diversity of gamelan groups around the world. Analyze enough sites to answer the following question. What type of gamelan is most prevalent (Javanese, Balinese, etc.)? For those groups that specify repertoire, does there seem to be a preference for contemporary or traditional pieces? What types of organizations sponsor these groups? How does this compare to what you have learned about sponsors for gamelan in Indonesia?*

Prominent Javanese performers—musicians, dancers, and *dhalangs*—have managed to shape transnational careers, thanks to this burgeoning interest in Javanese arts. Pak Cokro is not unique in this regard. Others include Hardja Susilo, the first to teach at an American university, as well as Sumarsam, Harjito, and Midiyanto, to name a few (see figures 8.2 and 8.3). Grants from private and government agencies have enabled various universities and community groups to invite guest artists for a year or more. These guest artists often perform with other ensembles, too, broadening the web of connections. Less frequently, Javanese groups tour outside Indonesia.

FIGURE 8.3 *Sumarsam has taught and performed at Wesleyan University since the 1970s and has earned a doctorate in ethnomusicology. He is shown wearing a traditional musician's jacket and head covering. (Photo by Bill Burkhart.)*

CONCLUSION

Extensive changes have occurred at home in Indonesia, too. The general economic crisis of the 1990s reduced performing opportunities. Training has also changed. The last musicians who were trained in the royal courts during their heyday have passed away, taking with them knowledge of the deeply *interconnected* court culture that regulated the *appropriateness* of *gendhing* to particular dramatic situations in *wayang kulit*, for instance. The first graduates of the government's high school conservatories and college-level academies are reaching retirement age. Fears voiced by some that formalized training at these institutions would lead to excessive standardization have not materialized, but anecdotal evidence points to a reduction in the scope of oral/aural knowledge and *flexibility* among younger performers even as technical mastery appears to have become more widespread. The relationship between arts institutions and other performers has shifted, too. On the one hand, higher education in the arts has been upgraded with many more musicians, dancers, and *dhalangs* studying toward advanced degrees; on the other, more compositional experimentation is taking place outside the academy than ever before.

The change that may have the longest effect is the surge in high-quality children's gamelan ensembles. I was astounded by a video Midiyanto showed me of the ensemble that trains at his house in Eromoko. These children, ranging from seven or eight to fourteen years of age, were not playing the simple *lancaran* that have been taught in schools for decades. Instead, Midiyanto had taught them harder pieces in complex arrangements more reminiscent of the style of the arts academy. They learn by focused training and rehearsal rather than the informal osmosis that has been typical. They play at a very high level, winning numerous competitions, but they are far from alone. The economic situation may still be grim and performance opportunities may not be as numerous now as ten years ago, but the next generation of gamelan musicians is arriving.

Glossary

ada-ada *dhalang's* song expressing tension or anger

alus refined

ayak-ayakan *gendhing lampah* for stately movement (usually used for gods and kings)

balungan melody usually played on the *saron*

bedhug largest barrel drum, struck with a mallet, used mainly in *gamelan sekatèn* and for certain dances

bonang gong chime

bonang panerus smaller gong chime

campursari literally "mixture of essences"; a popular genre mixing the instruments and musical practices of gamelan with those of Indonesian popular music

céngkok melodic formula leading to a *sèlèh*

ciblon medium-size drum

dangdut Indonesian popular music mixing Indian drumming with electric instruments

demung largest *saron*

dhalang puppet master in *wayang kulit*; the narrator in *wayang wong*

gambang xylophone

gamelan gadhon small gamelan consisting mainly of the softer-sounding instruments

gamelan sekatèn ceremonial palace gamelan with unusually large low-pitched instruments, played to celebrate the Prophet Muhammad's birth

gendèr tube-resonated metallophone with 12–14 keys, played with two padded mallets

gendèr panerus smaller *gendèr*, pitched one octave higher than the gendèr

gendhing gamelan piece

gendhing lampah pieces with dense colotomic structures for accompanying movement

gérong male chorus

gong ageng largest gong

gongan gong cycle

gong suwukan slightly smaller gong than the *gong ageng*

heterophony a musical texture consisting of two or more variants of a single melody played simultaneously

idiophone an instrument consisting of a rigid sounding body such as a gong or bell

imbal interlocking

irama rhythmic organization defined by the speed of the basic beat and its ratio to the fastest-moving parts

karawitan gamelan music

kasar coarse

kempul medium-size hanging gong

kempyang small high-pitched gong

kendhang drum

kendhang gendhing large drum

kendhang sabet medium-size drum played in *wayang*

kenong horizontally suspended, medium-pitched gong

kenongan phrase ending with a *kenong* stroke; usually one-half or one-fourth of a *gongan*

ketawang musical form based on 16-beat cycle, usually played at a slow tempo

kethuk small relatively low-pitched gong

ketipung small drum

klenèngan gamelan performance without dance or theater

kraton palace

kroncong Indonesian popular music deriving from centuries of mixing European and local elements

ladrang musical form based on 32-beat gong cycle

lancaran musical form based on 16-beat colotomic structure, usually played at a fast tempo

macapat type of poetry written to be sung

mipil *bonang* elaborating technique

monophonic describing a musical texture consisting of a single melody

musik music other than gamelan music

ngelik section of a piece in a high register (contrasts with the *umpak*)

ombak literally "wave"; the undulation in volume when a big gong sounds

panerusan elaborating instrument(s)

pathet act in *wayang kulit* and musical mode

pathetan *dhalang*'s song expressing calm

peking smallest *saron*

pélog seven-tone scale

pendhapa pavilion (see figure 1.2)

pesindhèn female singer

polyphonic describing a musical texture consisting of two or more distinct melodies played simultaneously

punakawan servant/companion figure in theater, often comical

rebab two-string bowed lute

salahan drum pattern for the end of a cycle

sampak *gendhing lampah* used for intense battles

saron trough-resonated metallophone played with a hard mallet

sekaran "flower" pattern leading to a *sèlèh*

sèlèh goal tone

sendhon *dhalang*'s song expressing sadness or confusion

siter zither

sléndro five-tone scale

slenthem tube-resonated metallophone played with a padded mallet

srepeg *gendhing lampah* for movement ranging from walking to fighting

suling end-blown bamboo flute

sulukan *dhalang*'s songs (see *ada-ada*, *pathetan*, and *sendhon*)

suwuk ending

talu sequence of pieces played as an overture to a *wayang* performance

tembang song, poem, or poetry

umpak basic section (contrasts with the *ngelik*)

wangsalan riddle; type of poetry sung by the *pesindhèn* consisting of a pair of 12-syllable lines

wayang kulit shadow play

wayang wong theater with human actors who also dance and sing and with narration by a *dhalang*; related to *wayang kulit*

References

Arps, Bernard. 1992. *Tembang in Two Traditions: Performance and Interpretation of Javanese Literature.* London: SOAS.

Becker, A.L. 1979. "Text-Building Epistemology and Aesthetics in Javanese Shadow Theatre." In *The Imagination of Reality: Essays in Southeast Asian Coherence Systems,* edited by A.L. Becker and Aram Yengoyan, pp. 211–43. Norwood, New Jersey: Ablex Publishers.

Becker, Judith. 1979. "Time and Tune in Java." In *The Imagination of Reality: Essays in Southeast Asian Coherence Systems,* edited by A.L. Becker and Aram Yengoyan, pp. 197–209. Norwood, New Jersey: Ablex Publishing Corporation.

———. 1980. *Traditional Music in Modern Java.* Honolulu: University of Hawaii Press.

——— and Alton Becker. 1981. "A Musical Icon: Power and Meaning in Javanese Gamelan Music." In *The Sign in Music and Literature,* edited by Wendy Steiner, pp. 203–28. Austin: University of Texas.

Brandon, James R. 1970. *On Thrones of Gold: Three Javanese Shadow Plays.* Cambridge, Massachusetts: Harvard University Press.

Brinner, Benjamin. 1995. *Knowing Music, Making Music: Javanese Gamelan and the Theory of Musical Competence and Interaction.* Chicago: University of Chicago Press.

Brown, Robert, E., and Andrew Toth. 1971. *Javanese Court Gamelan.* Vol. 1. Nonesuch Records.

Gold, Lisa. 2005. *Music in Bali: Experiencing Music, Expressing Culture.* New York: Oxford University Press.

Harrison, Lou. 1985. "Thoughts About Slippery Slendro." *Selected Reports in Ethnomusicology* 6:111–17.

Lord, Albert Bates. 2000. *The Singer of Tales.* Cambridge Mass.: Harvard University Press.

Martopangrawit, R.L. 1984. *Catatan-Catatan Pengetahuan Karawitan.* Translated in *Karawitan: Source Readings in Javanese Gamelan and Vocal Music.* Vol. 1, edited by Judith Becker and Alan H. Feinstein, pp. 1–244. Ann Arbor: Center for South and Southeast Asian Studies, The University of Michigan.

Perlman, Marc. 1998. "The Social Meanings of Modal Practices: Status, History and Pathet in Central Javanese Music." *Ethnomusicology* 42:45–80.

———. 2004. *Unplayed Melodies: Javanese Gamelan and the Genesis of Music Theory.* Berkeley: University of California Press.

Probohardjono, R.M. Kodrat. 1984. *Gendhing Jawa.* Translated in *Karawitan: Source Readings in Javanese Gamelan and Vocal Music.* Vol.1, edited by Judith Becker and Alan H. Feinstein, pp. 409–38. Ann Arbor: Center for South and Southeast Asian Studies, The University of Michigan.

Quigley, Sam. 1996. "The Raffles Gamelan at Claydon House." *Journal of the American Musical Instrument Society* 22:5–41. Available online at http://www3.primushost.com/~samq/claydon/index.htm.

Santosa. 2001. "Constructing Images in Javanese Gamelan Performances: Communicative Aspects Among Musicians and Audiences in Village Communities." Ph.D. dissertation, University of California, Berkeley.

Sears, Laurie. 1996. *Shadows of Empire: Colonial Discourse and Javanese Tales.* Durham: Duke University Press.

Siegel, James. 1986. *Solo in the New Order: Language and Hierarchy in an Indonesian City.* Princeton: Princeton University Press.

Sumarsam. 1995. *Gamelan: Cultural Interaction and Musical Development in Central Java.* Chicago: University of Chicago Press.

Supanggah, Rahayu. 2003. "Campur Sari: A Reflection." *Asian Music* 34/2:1–20.

Sutton, R. Anderson. 1991. *Traditions of Gamelan Music in Java.* Cambridge, UK: Cambridge University Press.

———. 2002. *Calling Back the Spirit: Music, Dance, and Cultural Politics in Lowland South Sulawesi.* Oxford, UK: Oxford University Press.

Sweeney, Amin. 1980. *Authors and Audiences.* Berkeley: University of California Center for South and Southeast Asia Studies. Monograph no. 20.

Vetter, Roger. n.d. *The Gamelans of the Kraton Yogyakarta.* Available online at http://web.grinnell.edu/courses/mus/gamelans/open.html.

Wade, Bonnie C. 2004. *Thinking Musically.* New York: Oxford University Press.

Weiss, Sarah 2006. *Listening to an Earlier Java: Aesthetics and Gender in Javanese Wayang.* Leiden: KITLV Press.

Resources

Reading

"Arts, Southeast Asian." Encyclopedia Britannica, 2005. Encyclopedia Britannica online at <http://search.eb.com/eb/article?tocId = 29587>.

Becker, Judith. 1991. "The Javanese Court Bedhaya Dance as a Tantric Analogy." In *Metaphor: A Musical Dimension*, edited by Jaime Kassler, pp. 109–20. Sydney, Australia: Currency Press.

———. 1993. *Gamelan Stories: Tantrism, Islam, and Aesthetics in Central Java.* Tempe: Program for Southeast Asian Studies, Arizona State University.

——— and Alan H. Feinstein, eds. 1984–1988. *Karawitan: Source Readings in Javanese Gamelan and Vocal Music.* 3 vols. Ann Arbor: University of Michigan Center for South and Southeast Asian Studies.

Brinner, Benjamin. 1989–1990. "At the Border of Sound and Silence: The Use and Function of Pathetan in Javanese Gamelan." *Asian Music* 21/1:1–34.

———. 1992. "Performer Interaction in a New Form of Javanese Wayang." In *Essays on Southeast Asian Performing Arts: Local Manifestations and Cross Cultural Implications*, edited by Kathy Foley, pp. 96–114. Berkeley: University of California at Berkeley Center for South and Southeast Asia Studies.

———. 1993. "A Musical Time Capsule from Java." *Journal of the American Musicological Society* 46/2:221–60.

———. 1993. "Freedom and Formulaity in the Suling Playing of Bapak Tarnopangrawit." *Asian Music* 24/2:1–38.

———. 1995. "Cultural Matrices and Innovation in Central Javanese Performing Arts." *Ethnomusicology* 39/3:433–56.

———. 1999. "Cognitive and Interpersonal Dimensions of Listening in Javanese Gamelan Performance." *The World of Music* 41/1:19–35.

Cooper, Nancy. 2000. "Singing and Silences: Transformations of Power Through Javanese Seduction Scenarios." *American Ethnologist* 27/3: 609–44.

Geertz, Clifford. 1976. *The Religion of Java.* Chicago: University of Chicago Press.

Hatch, Martin. 1986. "Social Change and the Functions of Music in Java." In *Explorations in Ethnomusicology: Essays in Honor of David P. McAllester,* edited by Charlotte J. Frisbie. Detroit, Michigan: Detroit Information Coordinators.

Keeler, Ward. 1987. *Javanese Shadow Plays, Javanese Selves*. Princeton, New Jersey: Princeton University Press.

———. 1992. *Javanese Shadow Puppets*. New York: Oxford University Press.

Koentjaraningrat. 1985. *Javanese Culture*. Singapore: Oxford University Press.

Lindsay, Jennifer. 1998. "Regionalism in Literature." In *Indonesian Heritage: Languages and Literature*, edited by John McGlynn, pp. 128–29. Singapore: Archipelago Press.

McGlynn, John, ed. 1998. *Indonesian Heritage: Languages and Literature*. Singapore: Archipelago Press.

Mrazek, Jan, ed. 2002. *Puppet Theater in Contemporary Indonesia: New Approaches to Performing Events*. Ann Arbor: University of Michigan Press. Michigan Papers on South and Southeast Asia, no. 50.

Pemberton, John. 1994. *On the Subject of "Java."* Ithaca: Cornell University Press.

Perlman, Marc. 1997. "Conflicting Interpretations: Indigenous Analysis and Historical Change in Central Javanese Music." *Asian Music* 38/1: 115–40.

——— and Carol L. Krumhansl. 1996. "An Experimental Study of Internal Interval Standards in Javanese and Western Musicians." *Music Perception* 14/2:95–116.

Quigley, Sam. "Gong Smithing in Twentieth Century Surakarta," available at http://www3.primushost.com/~samq/sackler/index.htm; photos of various gamelans available at http://www3.primushost.com/~samq/ensembles/ensembles.htm

Ricklefs, M.C. 1993. *A History of Modern Indonesia Since c. 1300*. Stanford: Stanford University Press.

Supanggah, Rahayu. 2004."Gatra: A Basic Concept of Traditional Javanese Gending." *Balungan* 9–10:1–11.

Sutton, R. Anderson. 1979. "Concept and Treatment in Javanese Gamelan Music, with Reference to the Gambang." *Asian Music* 11/1:59–79.

———. 1984. "Change and Ambiguity: Gamelan Style and Regional Identity in Yogyakarta." In *Aesthetic Tradition and Cultural Transition in Java and Bali,* edited by Stephanie Morgan and Laurie Jo Sears, pp. 221–46. Madison: University of Wisconsin Center for Southeast Asian Studies.

———. 1984. "Who Is the Pesindhen? Notes on the Female Singing Tradition in Java." *Indonesia* 37:119–34.

———. 1985. "Commercial Cassette Recordings of Traditional Music in Java: Implications for Performers and Scholars." *World of Music* 27/3:23–43.

———. 1985. "Musical Pluralism in Java: Three Local Traditions." *Ethnomusicology* 29/1:56–85.

———. 1987. "Variation and Composition in Java." *Yearbook for Traditional Music* 19:65–95.

———. 1997. "Humor, Mischief, and Aesthetics in Javanese Gamelan Music." *The Journal of Musicology* 15/3:390–415.

———, Suanda, Endo, and Sean Williams. 1998. "Java," In *Southeast Asia: The Garland Encyclopedia of World Music*. Vol. 4, edited by Terry Miller and Sean Williams, pp. 630–728. New York: Garland Publishing.

Weiss, Sarah. 2002. "Gender(ed) Aesthetics: Domains of Knowledge and 'Inherent' Dichotomies in Central Javanese Wayang Accompaniment." In *Puppet Theatre in Contemporary Indonesia: New Approaches to Javanese Wayang*, edited by Jan Mrazek, pp. 286–304. Ann Arbor: University of Michigan Press.

———. 2003. "*Kothong Nanging Kebak*, Empty Yet Full: Some Thoughts on Embodiment and Aesthetics in Javanese Performance." *Asian Music* 34/2:21–49.

Williams, Walter L. 1990. *Javanese Lives: Women and Men in Modern Indonesian Society*. New Brunswick: Rutgers University Press.

Listening

Chamber Music of Central Java. King Record KICC 5152.

Court Music of Kraton Surakarta. King Record KICC 5151. Accompaniment to one *srimpi* dance.

Dewa Ruci, een Javaans Schimmenspel. VPRO EW 9523. Short *wayang* performed in Holland by top *dhalang*, extensive liner notes.

Gamelan of Central Java: II. Ceremonial Music. Yantra Productions. Dunya Records. Felmay, 2002.

Gendhing Bonang/Court Music of Surakarta III. King Record KICC5238. Two long ceremonial pieces.

Javanese Court Gamelan. 3 vol. Elektra/Nonesuch 972044.

Klenengan Session of Solonese Gamelan I. King Record KICC 5185.

Music of Indonesia, Vol. 2: Indonesian Popular Music: Kroncong, Dangdut, and Langgam Jawa. Smithsonian Folkways Recordings, 1991. SFW40056.

Music of Mangkunegaran Solo. 2 vols. King Record KICC 5184 and 5194.

Royal Palace of Yogyakarta. 4 vols. Ocora C 560067–9 and 560087.

Shadow Music of Java. Rounder Records 5060 (features Ki Sutino Hardokocarito and Hardo Budoyo).

The Music of K.R.T. Wasitodiningrat. CMP Records 3007.

Viewing

Quigley, Sam. "Copper, Tin & Fire: Gongsmithing in Java. 1989. Available at http://www3.primushost.com/~samq/video/video.htm.

Widiyanto, S. Putro. *The Prosperity of Wibisana: A Performance of Javanese Wayang Kulit*. Portland, Oregon: Resonance Media, 1995.

————. *The Prosperity of Wibisana: A Study Guide and Analysis for the Javanese Wayang Kulit.* Portland, Oregon: Resonance Media, 1995.

Internet Sites

American Gamelan Institute has directories of gamelan ensembles, a catalog of publications and recordings for sale, the *kepatihan* notation font (a free download), podcasts, and links to other gamelan-related resources around the world. Available at www.gamelan.org

Gamelan notation and glossary. calarts.edu/~drummond/gendhing.html

Joglosemar Online has numerous pages on Central Javanese palaces, beliefs, festivals, dance, theater, and music. Available at www.joglosemar.co.id/joglo_index.html

Photos of Javanese dancers from the 1930s under the subject headings "gamelan" and "dancers—Indonesia." Available at digitalgallery.nypl.org/nypldigital/

Virtual gamelan allows user to hear and see "Lancaran Ricik-ricik" and "Ladrang Pangkur." Buttons at lower left give access to different visual representations: an interactive photo of a gamelan on which individual gongs and keys light up as they are sounded; a geometrical "translation" of the colotomic structure; and a graphic "score" of the piece which the user can alter to "compose" a piece. Available at www.cite-musique.fr/gamelan/shock.html

Virtual instrument museum with numerous examples of Javanese instruments including video clips of Sumarsam playing *gendèr, ciblon,* etc. Available at learningobjects.wesleyan.edu/vim/

Index

CD indicates track on compact disk, *a* indicates activity, and *f* indicates figure.